LOOKING DOWN ON WAR
AXIS WARSHIPS

DEDICATION

To Paul LaBar:

Naval Officer, Photo Scientist, superlative manager, teacher, mentor,

and the best boss I ever worked for.

LOOKING DOWN ON WAR
AXIS WARSHIPS
AS SEEN ON PHOTOS FROM ALLIED INTELLIGENCE FILES

Colonel Roy M. Stanley II, USAF (ret.)

Pen & Sword
MARITIME

Other Books by the Author

World War II Photo Intelligence

Prelude To Pearl Harbor

To Fool A Glass Eye

Asia From Above

V-Weapons Hunt

First published in Great Britain in 2011 by
PEN & SWORD MARITIME
An imprint of
Pen & Sword Books Ltd
47 Church Street
Barnsley
South Yorkshire
S70 2AS

ISBN 978 184884 471 1

Pen & Sword Books Ltd incorporates the Imprints of Pen & Sword Aviation,
Pen & Sword Family History, Pen & Sword Maritime, Pen & Sword Military,
Wharncliffe Local History, Pen & Sword Select, Pen & Sword Military Classics, Leo Cooper,
Remember When, Seaforth Publishing and Frontline Publishing

For a complete list of Pen & Sword titles please contact
PEN & SWORD BOOKS LIMITED
47 Church Street, Barnsley, South Yorkshire, S70 2AS, England
E-mail: enquiries@pen-and-sword.co.uk

Website: www.pen-and-sword.co.uk

TABLE OF CONTENTS

INTRODUCTION

This book isn't designed to rehash the minutia of these fighting vessels or discuss, except incidentally, how the ships were handled, miss-handled, or deployed. There are plenty of naval experts who know more about those things than I. There are also many excellent books that go into detail on construction, manning, equipment, performance and history of all the significant warships—mostly based upon post-war "ground truth." Some of the ones I like best are cited in this Bibliography, and I really made use of them. They provided good firsthand accounts and very good historical analysis, but that isn't what Allied Intelligence had to do in WW II, and that's not what I'm trying to do.

It's my intent to provide an informed reader a supplement to those authoritative books: a look at the Axis Navies through the aerial and ground photos Allied Intelligence had to locate, identify and track various enemy naval units, to tell what they were capable of and what they might do. Thousands of photos like the ones that follow, along with reports from agents on the ground plus hundreds of thousands of intercepted communications and electronic emanations, made up what the Allies knew during WW II.[1] They had to interpret the information on those photos trying to understand what was going on "on the other side of the hill." Sometimes I know what the Allies knew, sometimes I was in the same boat as the analysts (forgive the jest), with only the photos and photo interpreter training to steer my insight. On the trip to the end of the book I'll tell you what those images say to me now.

I didn't seek these photos out—in a way, they found me during my assignment as Deputy in the DoD organization holding all aerial imagery files, including Army, Navy and Allied source photographs from World War II. Our Division came under pressure from on high to destroy dormant holdings to reduce storage space and cost. The boss, Paul LaBar, and I were loath to destroy those dust coated boxes without knowing what was in them.

During lunch breaks, and staying after work, I looked through the materials as fast as I could, trying to learn if those boxes contained anything of historical value. Almost immediately I began to find gems, nearly all them from "the Big War." One box could hold four or five old metal cans, each containing anywhere from 100' to 500' of original or duplicate roll negatives. Boxes with cut film, i.e. single or groups of negatives someone had decided were important or useful years before, could hold as many as a thousand items ranging from 4" x 5" or 5" x 7" RAF negatives to U.S. standard aerial film negatives with 9" x 9" or 9" x 18" exposures—even dozens of boxes with the surprising find of tens of thousands of captured original German 12" x 12" positive paper prints.[2] I quickly learned that many of those cut-negatives (individual frames copied from roll aerial film or single ground shots) originated in WW II briefing materials or publications, many created on copy cameras so they would be available to a broader audience later. That meant most of them began as selected materials but few had much to identify their importance forty years later—to evaluate them I had to understand them. For some it was easy, not so for others.

My initial photo interpreter (PI) training was on WW II and Korean War prints and I was completely at home with the material I was finding. But my initial "for real" PI was on prints[3] covering China, Korea and Southeast Asia, so I had no occasion to go into "heavy warships." I started finding them on the film and cut-negatives I was reviewing and found them fascinating. Much of the film came from U.S. sources but many of the cut-negatives in particular obviously originated with the RAF. I grew up during WW II and have an academic background in history, so I quickly found

6

researching original sources from that era addictive. The things learned resulted in my first book, and sent me on a voyage of discovery, reliving World War II through aerial photography—a voyage that continues to this day. It led me into a gratifying process of learning about the geography, technology and equipment necessary to understand combat in 1939-1945.

I found major warships fun to PI because with a few good reference works, such as <u>Jane's Fighting Ships</u>, you can easily identify a class and often the name of the vessel, even on small-scale imagery. One of the first rolls of old film I reviewed was 1942 RAF coverage of the Port of Gdynia (Gotenhafen). Scanning the quays I will never forget seeing what was obviously a large warship, but its measurements and shape didn't match anything I could find in any reference. It was without guns, though barbettes for turrets were apparent, and it sported a "funny" bow. The location of the warship precluded something under construction. Looking farther afield in the same port I spotted what looked for all the world like an aircraft carrier. Remember this was thirty years ago, before many of the most useful WW II reference books came out and before all the sources readily available on the internet—books of the day didn't print many photos and fewer still aerial photos. I didn't know the Germans ever tried to build a carrier, but there it was, up a side channel and apparently abandoned. I had to know what those ships were. I was hooked.

Those images drew me into research to identify what I was seeing—which in this case turned out to be the Battlecruiser *Gneisenau* in the process of being decommissioned. The temporary bow was needed because of battle damage. The carrier was the never-finished *Graf Zeppelin*. Almost all the photos in this book came from my quest for a way to understand and best dispose of a priceless imagery collection that had lain dormant for over two decades and was under pressure for arbitrary destruction to save space and money.

Presented here are selected images of the German, Italian, French and Japanese navies from retired U.S. Intelligence files, many of them never published before and some not in our possession until late in, or even after, the war. They show the Axis Navies as Allied Intelligence analysts knew them.

By the way, I will sometimes use standard Intel abbreviations for warships: BB = battleship (main guns above 11" in caliber); BC = Battlecruiser; CA = heavy cruiser (8" main guns); CL = light cruiser (6" main guns or smaller caliber); DD = destroyer; DDE = destroyer escort or patrol vessel; SS = submarine; CV = aircraft carrier, CVL = light carrier, CVE = escort carrier, AV = aircraft/seaplane tender.

Other abbreviations you'll run into are: ONI (USN Office of Naval Intelligence); RDF or simply DF (radio direction finding—using emitted signals to triangulate a location); USAAF (United States Army Air Force); RAF (Royal Air Force); PR (aerial photoreconnaissance); PI (photo interpretation) and SIGINT (Signals Intelligence, the interception, and if necessary, decoding/decryption, of enemy radio traffic).

The opinions expressed in these pages are those of an old imagery and Intelligence analyist and based primarily upon the materials presented in the book. The way I learned to PI, you were like a referee or umpire, "calling 'em like you see 'em," and that's what I've done here, but I don't pretend to be infallible in my judgments.

A final note: if you don't always see things I refer to on an image, remember that I viewed the photos closer to the original using computer magnification and/or precision optics, so I saw them larger and sharper than they could ever be reproduced in a published work. Trust me, if I tell you something is there, it's there. You'd be amazed what an experienced PI can see given sufficient time…and a steady supply of Single Malt Scotch.

7

FOOTNOTES

[1]Analysts at the time culled what came in each month, searching for the spectacular, unusual or informative for publication in their magazines. We used to call those photos "happy snaps." Publication resulted in negs that were then filed for subsequent reproduction if necessary—and those are many of the ones I found.

[2]The retrieval indexes were long gone, so much of what I found was unidentified as to date and location, but items of obvious significance and provenance were subsequently turned over to the appropriate divisions of the U.S. National Archives.

[3]When I began my career as a PI the USAF was gradually transitioning to use of roll film positives for interpretation.

CHAPTER I
BACKGROUND

Prior to World War II German warship numbers, types, sizes and armaments were severely limited by the Treaty of Versailles that ended World War I. Numbers and tonnages of naval ships of the United States, Great Britain, the Empire of Japan, the Kingdom of Italy and the French Third Republic were nominally limited by the Washington Naval Treaty of 1922 and various follow-on agreements of 1930 and 1936. As Hitler gained control of Germany he wanted to be on a par with the "victorious powers." Japan pulled out of the treaty agreements in the mid-1930s and Italy was secretly violating them. As the threat of another war loomed, each nation began rearming, pushing the Treaty Limits hard.

Of course each European nation wanted to stay ahead of Germany, Italy and each other (with Japan being something of an enigma). There was an increasing trend for tonnage and main battery size to "cheat" on those limitations and the closer war became, the more blatant the "cheating." Each nation wanted the most powerful ships in each class and numbers sufficient to deter or prevail in any conflict. The Depression severely limited funds available, so everyone wanted the most ship for the money and some innovative designs resulted. Of course the Naval Intelligence organizations of each nation worked overtly and covertly to determine what friends and potential adversaries were doing in their shipyards and fitting-out docks.

For "European nations" the Gold Standard was Britain's Royal Navy and it was watched accordingly by potential enemies. That was slightly less true in the Pacific where, to Japan's annoyance, the United States Navy was dominant, at least on paper.

Oben: **Die englische Flotte im Hafen von Gibraltar.**
A = Schlachtschiff „*Rodney*" oder „*Nelson*",
B = Schlachtschiffe der „*Malaya*"-Klasse
    (z. T. heute umgebaut wie „Warspite"),
C = Schlachtkreuzer „*Hood*" (Schlachtschiff!),
D = Schwere Kreuzer der „*Dorsetshire*"-Klasse,
E = Leichte Kreuzer der „*Leander*"-Klasse,
F = Leichte Kreuzer der „*Ceres*"-Klasse
    (z. T. heute als Flugabwehrkreuzer umgebaut),
G = Jeweils 2 Zerstörer der „*H*"-Klasse,
H = Netzleger „*Guardian*".

Unten: **Reserveflotte in Portland.**
A = Leichte Kreuzer der **C-Klasse**: „*Ceres*"und„*Cardiff*",
    4290 ts, 29 Kn.
B = Minenkreuzer „***Adventure***", 6740 ts, 27,7 Kn.
C = Leichter Kreuzer „***Effingham***", 9770 ts, 30,5 Kn.
D = Leichter Kreuzer der **D-Klasse**, 4850 ts, 29 Kn.

Im Hintergrund Zerstörer der **H-Klasse** (gleich lange Schornsteine!), rechts hinten „**V**"- und „**W**"-Klasse (dünner langer Schornstein, dahinter kurzer dicker Schornstein).

Spithead Reede, *ältere Aufnahme (1935)*
im Hintergrund Portsmouth

linke Bildhälfte			*rechte Bildhälfte*		

Im Hintergrund verteilt Zerstörer der „A-D"-Klasse.

		„Victoria	4 Schwere Kreuzer (3 Schornsteine!) der „London"-Klasse
Schlachtkreuzer „Hood"	*„Iron Duke"*	*and*	*S.S. „Resolution" S.S. „Royal Sovereign" S.S. „Ramillies"¹)*
		Albert"	

3 Zerstörer „A-D"-Klasse — *L.Krz. „C"- S.S. „Queen Elizabeth"- S.S. „Queen Elizabeth"-Klasse Klasse¹) Klasse¹)*

L. Krz. „D"-Klasse L. Krz. „D"-Klasse¹) — *L. Krz. „C"-Klasse¹) L. Krz. „Hawkins"-Klasse L. Krz. „Hawkins"-Klasse*

großer Frachter (etwa 10 000 BRT) d. Royal Mail L. — *Kanaldampfer „Amsterdam"-Klasse größerer (französischer?) (Fahrgast)Dampfer, etwa 12 000 BRT.*

¹) *Diese Schiffe wirken trotz größerer Nähe zum Beschauer unverhältnismäßig klein (Anstrich, Winkellage).*

Zerstörer und **Kanonenboote** *der englischen Reserveflotte vor dem Hafen von Portland (Weymouth).*
Erste Reihe von der Mitte nach links: Kanonenboote.
Erste Reihe von der Mitte nach rechts und dahinter: Zerstörer der „A"- bis „I"-Klasse.
Im Vordergrund: Je ein leichter Kreuzer der „C"- und „D"-Klasse.

Weymouth *(1938)*

links		*rechts*
Zerstörer	*S. Krz. „London"-Klasse*	
„A-I"-	*S. S. „Resolution"*	*S. S. „Royal*
Klasse	*S. S. „Ramillies"¹)*	*Sovereign"*
	S. S. „Rodney"	*S. S. „Ramillies"¹)*
	Flgzg.-Träg. „Glorious"	*S. S. „Nelson"*
	L. Krz. „Southampton"	*älterer Zerstörer*
	¹) oder „Royal Oak".	

All of these photos are from a German manual on the Royal Navy. The photos themselves probably originated in "open source" literature (newspapers, magazines, postcards and books) but they give an indication of the sheer size of the navy a potential enemy of Britain faced. Going into the pre-war build-up, Germany had nothing remotely comparable, and neither did Italy. In that era France's formidable fleet was not viewed as a threat by its World War I comrade-in-arms.

11

Enforced scrapping of most of its earlier warships from battleships to submarines turned out to be an advantage for Germany. Those ships would have been badly obsolete by 1939 and it gave them the opportunity to start building afresh. Severe limits on displacement, guns and ship types forced a carefully controlled excellence in rebuilding. As a result, Germany launched some of the most powerful, efficient and most aesthetically appealing vessels of the war. Using the latest technology in design, construction, power plants and armament, these ships were almost universally fast, well protected and packed a terrific punch. If they had a flaw it was weakness resulting from being on the "cutting edge" of ship design and construction. For example, the use of diesel motors, welded hulls and relatively light main batteries were intended to save weight and get the maximum ship inside (or near) Treaty limitations—but they didn't always work as well as hoped. Their designs also suffered from a lack of German deep water experience, resulting in handling problems in the open Atlantic and retrofit of bows on the larger ships. A third limitation, one that Nazi German suffered in many areas throughout the war, was that they simply could not produce and man enough combat ships to meet opponents beyond occasional local superiority.

Planners in Germany knew their surface ships had stumbled in surface confrontations with the Royal Navy during The Great War, but their submarines had almost brought Britain to its knees. They knew the Atlantic was England's life line and they intended to sever it this time using commerce raiders as well as submarines. Germany's edge was they only had to arm to meet one fleet while the Royal Navy had the expensive task of having credible strength in both oceans and the Mediterranean. Treaty limitations, costs allowed, and the Depression forced Britain to keep earlier warships so she entered the war with many older battleships, battlecruisers and cruisers that were well-gunned but light on armor and relatively slow. Those were the ships that the Axis navies aimed to counter. France never intended to fight ally England at sea but was wary of the German and Italian ships being made and concentrated on the Mediterranean. Similarly, the Italian Navy was mainly concerned about operations in the Med. This gave Germany, Italy and France an edge in ship design, since range and duration at sea weren't particular problems. Of course quite the opposite was true for the Royal Navy, Japan and the United States.

Well into the 1930s, big gun warships were still viewed as the kings of the sea and their very size meant there were only certain shipyards with building-ways, drydocks and cranes large enough for them to be built and supported. The same size-factor made it impossible (except in Japan) to hide a major warship from prying eyes. That meant pre-WW II naval construction became an "arms race" carefully observed and reported by agents and Attachés from other nations. Most nations went to great lengths to hide what they could and cheat wherever possible. Much of the crucial information on capabilities could only be guessed and some of the "guessers" were less adept than others. Since everyone was spying, and the ships afloat were impossible to hide, the only real secrets were the actual tonnage, potential speed and range, and technical innovations that might not be obvious. Indeed, the launching of a major warship itself was usually a major propaganda event, attended by dignitaries of many nations. In the inter-war years warships were also a subject of great interest to many people from model-makers through "old salts" to those concerned about the state of the peace, so there were a host of civilian ship-watchers publishing works such as Jane's Fighting Ships, with photos, drawings and ship specifications along with as much about capabilities as could be known or guessed from overt observation.

Of course each nation also had Naval Attachés (legal spies) visiting the other's ports and using every opportunity to pick up scraps of information and report on each new construction. It is amazing how much can be learned at Embassy cocktail parties after a few drinks. Another source of inside information was workers or even low-level Naval Officers involved with the ships and puffed-up with the "I've got a secret" syndrome. Give them a little encouragement, a little flattery, and they'd brag

12

about what they knew. Then there were occasions when Allied or Axis warships put into a foreign port and experts got a better look, doing their best to assess the less obvious capabilities of the visitor. One example of this was when the new German "Pocket Battleship" *Admiral Graf Spee* was sent to Spithead Roads to honor King George VI's Coronation. A new class of warship, *Spee* had been commissioned just 18 months earlier and was thought to be the best of the three.

Naval Intelligence offices in each nation meticulously pieced together thousands of tiny scraps of information trying to produce understanding. They kept track of what each of the other nations were building and where, and followed the locations of all the major warships that were operational. The big question on each ship was still its capability; offensive and defensive power, fire control, armor, speed and cruising range.

Once war began, a veil of secrecy dropped on such overt intelligence opportunities to monitor German warships. The Italian and the French Navies were quickly pulled behind that veil (Japanese ships had been hidden from view since 1937). Risk to Britain's lifeline of Atlantic convoys made it of paramount importance for the British and Commonwealth Navies (and later the U.S. Navy), to know the whereabouts of major threat warships and to learn what was being built as the Axis powers threw off all pretense of limitations on warship types, numbers, tonnage and armament. In the Atlantic, surface raiders were the initial concern as German submarines were few, of limited capability, and had a dangerous out-and-back passage between German ports and the open sea.

Following the movements of major ships in the Atlantic or Med was like a chess game played on a grand scale but with no assurance that you see every move. Fortunately, there were only certain moves possible with only certain ports able to host the big warships. Of course the ports where the big ships were made (or currently under construction) were known from pre-war information. Signals Intelligence and agents reported where the ships went for exercises and crew training. For Germany the principle ports were Kiel, Hamburg, Bremen and Wilhelmshaven—all but Kiel opening onto narrow waters dominated by Great Britain. Once they occupied Poland, the Kriegsmarine also used Baltic ports beyond easy reach of the RAF for repair, training and basing of major naval units, mainly the complex of Gdynia (Gotenhafen) and Gdansk (Danzig).

Ships under construction were not a current threat, but those fitting out and commissioned were, and it was important to watch progress to determine when a warship would become a threat. Length and weight of the big ships meant there were few places to search with limited Intelligence means and resources available. Agent reports from the Continent were invaluable but took far too long to reach England to be reliable in maintaining an accurate Naval Order of Battle (NOB). Radio Direction Finding (RDF) was an excellent way to track a warship by triangulating transmissions—if the ship was transmitting and if the transmission wasn't a ruse from another ship or shore station. The very "close hold" system of interception and decoding/decryption of enemy message traffic was in its infancy in 1940 and only useful if something was mentioned about a ship location or movement. The only collection source that could specifically target an intelligence objective (such as a port or capital ship) and rapidly achieve positive results was aerial photoreconnaissance, but RAF resources to accomplish those hazardous single aircraft missions were also extremely limited and in demand for many competing requirements.

Emphasizing the British concern over the German Navy, just hours after war was declared in September 1939, the RAF sent a reconnaissance Blenheim to report on the German fleet at Wilhelmshaven with only partial observation resulting. Returning the next day the same Blenheim and pilot photographed German warships in Schilling Roads and the RAF mounted a strike which "brought shocking proof that the excellent Blenheim was not suitable for daylight bombing against heavily defended targets, and there were tragic losses"(Air Spy, p. 15-16). The same limitations negated the Blenheim's capability to perform photoreconnaissance over other defended enemy ports

13

(or any defended target for that matter). The Blenheim couldn't reach the speeds and altitudes necessary to survive in enemy airspace, and at its highest altitude the cameras, lenses and film were malfunctioning from cold. Intelligence data on Axis warships began to grow stale until the advent of photo reconnaissance operations by Sidney Cotton's Special Survey Flight[1] with Spitfires modified for maximum speed, range and altitude, and providing heat to camera lenses and film.

One of the most important recon tasks was to collect regular aerial photo coverage of all the key enemy ports. Even before the more dramatic threat of the Blitz in the summer and fall of 1940, enemy submarines and surface raiders were a serious threat to Britain's capacity to wage a protracted war. The danger of surface attacks on Allied convoys gradually faded but that from submarines steadily increased throughout the war. The number of ports servicing and housing subs grew considerably as the Germans gained control of Europe. While U-boats (*Unterseeboots*) were based where they could get out into the Atlantic with a shorter, safer passage, many German surface ships were moved to Baltic ports further from the reach of RAF Bomber Command.

RAF photoreconnaissance aircraft evolved to greater speed, altitude and range, by late 1940 no Axis port was out of range. Fortunately, the major warships from battleships to light cruisers were hard to hide and extremely easy to identify down to a specific vessel, even given the extremely small scale of many of the images collected.

Of course submarines regularly leaving German bases in occupied France (Brest, Le Havre, Lorient, Cherbourg, St. Nazaire), magnified the sub-threat immeasurably because they permitted Atlantic sorties of longer duration and subs based there were harder to track and interdict. Major Axis surface ships didn't move around much. They didn't have to. Their potential power as commerce raiders was a formidable threat in being, made credible by sorties early in the war. The Allies were forced to keep matching warships in stations suitable for intercepting Axis vessels should they sortie against Atlantic or Mediterranean convoys, effectively taking those Allied warships out of the game without combat.

Agents in occupied Europe reported on warships arriving at a location. Allied RDF was also particularly useful in locating warships moving or hiding at a new location, often triggering a PR flight to confirm the Intel. RDF was a major tool for locating ships at sea, particularly submarines. Once located, aerial photos were useful to keep track of surface ship whereabouts—or at least verify that it hadn't surreptitiously moved again. Weather permitting; it was not unusual for aerial coverage of a port to occur daily, monitoring the most dangerous warships. For example, missions from Scotland would routinely fly along the Baltic coast taking pictures of Königsberg, Gdynia, Gdansk and other targets along the way (such as the V-weapons development center at Peenemunde). Other photo missions flown from southern England would cover Kiel, Brunsbüttel, the Kiel Canal, Wilhelmshaven, Hamburg's shipyards, and French ports known to harbor major warships or submarines. Photo missions from Gibraltar, Egypt and Malta watched the French and Italian fleets.

Smaller ships, often consorts of the major capitol ships, had many more locations where they could berth, but their combat power was also less so following them was not as intense a focus—frequently a serendipitous result of looking for the "big fellows."

Allied aerial photoreconnaissance also monitored the building of enemy warships—with emphasis on submarines since they posed the greatest threat. Analysts watched construction methods and looked for new types that might have new capabilities. Monitoring everything to do with Axis submarines became a separate field of expertise that got increasingly better throughout the war.

As we shall see later, understanding and keeping track of warships of the Imperial Japanese Navy was an entirely different matter.

FOOTNOTE

[1]Which quickly grew into the Photographic Reconnaissance Unit (PRU) then later, 541Sq. See my books World War II Photo Reconnaissance and V-Weapons Hunt for the PRU story.

CHAPTER II

NAVAL BASES, PORTS & HARBORS

Because of their length and burden, major naval units are limited in where they can berth for reprovisioning and/or repair. They might visit a smaller port but must be based at a large port or Naval Base with sufficient facilities. It is impossible to keep such bases a secret so spies and Naval Attachés knew just where to look for the big gun ships. It was important for each Intelligence Service to remain aware of places where the most dangerous warships could harbor—to get a better look at them and follow their movements. Here are examples of the type of "open source" items voraciously gleaned from several potentially hostile countries before the war. Agents, tourists, people screening books and magazines and Military Attachés in embassies all over the world collected anything and everything that might be useful. This stream of gems and trivia was forwarded to London and Washington and dutifully filed by the essentially librarial intelligence organizations of the day. Once war began, aerial imagery was the main visual source.

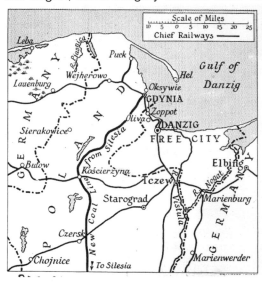

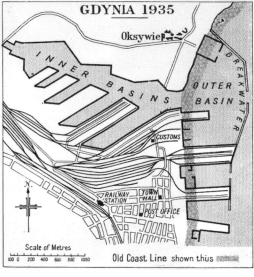

AREA 12—POLAND—R—*.—GDYNIA.—SKETCH MAPS SHOWING INNER AND OUTER BASINS, BREAKWATER, RAILWAY STATION, CUSTOMS, TOWN HALL, POST OFFICE, ETC. 1935—MIS NY 7748—M5475 E1832—*.—

AREA 12—POLAND RESTRICTED—*.—GDYNIA—HARBOR—900,332 CFL—N1832 W1832

Of considerably greater significance were photos like the hammer-head crane (right), photographed at Danzig's Schichau Shipyard in 1926. It was 60 meters high and could lift 250 tons, giving an idea of what might be accomplished at that yard.

Cranes of this size were vital to handling items such as large machinery, boilers, propellers and shafts, sections of armor plate, gun-barrels, turrets and prefabricated sections of the "heavy ships."

After German occupation of Poland in 1939, Gdynia was renamed Gotenhafen and the Danzig-Gdynia complex was considered "safe." It became a major Reichsmarine center for ship building, ship repair, ship basing and crew training. Along with Kiel, German naval

SA.618   Neg.N93198
ATTACK ON GDYNIA
9.10.43
APPROXIMATE BOMB PLOT
• Position of well defined bursts
///, Areas of heavy concentration.
Photographic background 7.10.43 N/949-205

strength and activity in this area made the Baltic "Unser Meer" (with apologies to Mussolini).

Once general war began, many sources of intelligence dried up or slowed down but aerial photo reconnaissance (PR) flourished. Able to go almost anywhere any time (weather permitting), PR made it possible to watch ports and harbors and capture what was going in at several places in close time proximity to avoid "double counting" something. That Intelligence collection capability made it possible to follow the location of significant ships.

(Left) Despite being 350 miles east of Kiel, Gdynia was not immune from bombing.

RAF 540Sq Mosquitoes from Leuchars in Scotland were particularly effective in covering the Baltic ports from Kiel to Königsberg (Kaliningrad).

LEGEND
1. Liner DEUTSCHLAND type
2. Liner STUTTGART.
3. Floating crane.
4. Tender 180'
5. M/V 300/350'
6. Vessel 100/150'
7. M/V 250' possible Sperrbrecher
8. Auxiliary 250'
9. Liner CAP ARCONA
10. Coaster
11. Ex-SCHLESIEN battleship.
12. M/V 250/300'

(Above) Vertical coverage of Danzig (Gdansk), Poland on 12 December 1942. Sharp eyes will find the aircraft (probably a JU 88) caught in flight on the Danzig imagery—enlargement is at right. It might be an accident or it might be a Luftwaffe plane "pacing" the high-flying RAF Mosquito.

17

Danzig showed a lot of activity in the fall of 1944. Ships of Destroyer Escort size or smaller were being built or repaired all along the left bank of the waterway curving around the central island. There are at least seventeen submarines in the fan-shaped waters at upper right. At least five more subs are in drydocks near the smaller fan shaped inlet at center left, and one is apparently moored in mid-river.

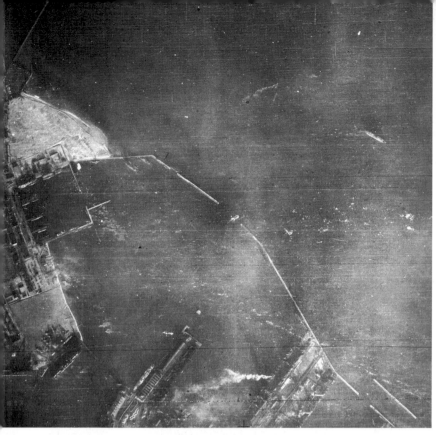

RAF sortie N680 on 12 December 1942 also imaged the Outer Harbor at Gdynia in occupied Poland. The rectangular area at upper left is the submarine base, showing little activity at this time. At lower right are at least four large merchant ships, one a passenger liner (note lifeboats), sheltering in port for the duration of the war.

(Left) Gdynia's Inner Harbor on 24 March 1945. Soviet ground forces were nearing and every ship that could move has been sailed off or sunk as a blockship as this major German Baltic Naval Base Gdynia was abandoned. The rail yard is jammed with cars.

I've left the close-spaced images to show what typical RAF PR roll film coverage looked like.

Imagery of 20 August 1942 (above) shows Gdynia's Inner and Outer Harbors in more active days. The quays and moles are lined with commercial ships and an occasional warship. Battlecruisers *Scharnhorst* and *Gneisenau* are here to repair damage incurred during the "Channel Dash." (more on them in the next chapter). Curiously, the large rail yards are almost empty of traffic.

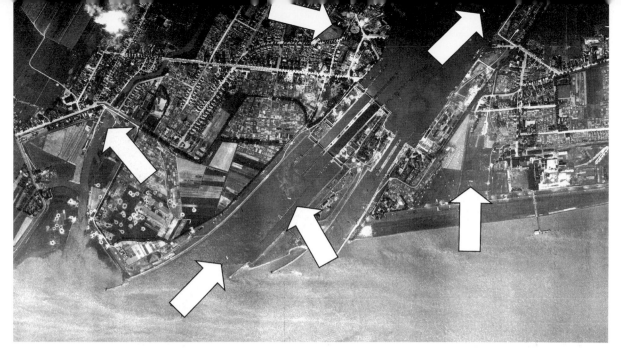

Important naval facilities had to be protected by active and passive defenses. Fighter planes, anti-aircraft artillery, barrage balloons, decoys, smoke and camouflage were some of the methods used. None of them were able to deflect or stop raids by heavy bombers.

This is Brunsbüttel, the southwest end of the Kiel Canal early in the war. It isn't either a port or naval base, but was critical to German shipping, permitting movement between the Elbe Estuary and Kiel on the Baltic without a long exposed transit of Denmark. Arrows show some of many barrage balloons passively defending those important locks. Some bombing has occurred, but was wide of the mark at lower left.While camouflage might work for individual installations, waterways, ports and other naval facilities were too large and too well-known to disguise. Nor could they be effectively defended as point targets by AAA (such as a factory complex). It was finally realized that the only alternative was to make it impossible or difficult for a bomb-aimer to acquire the target visually. One answer was smoke generators burning a fuel-oil mixture giving off dense white smoke that stayed close to the ground. This generator is in Norway and had German destroyers in the background. One can only imagine the risk braved to get this picture.

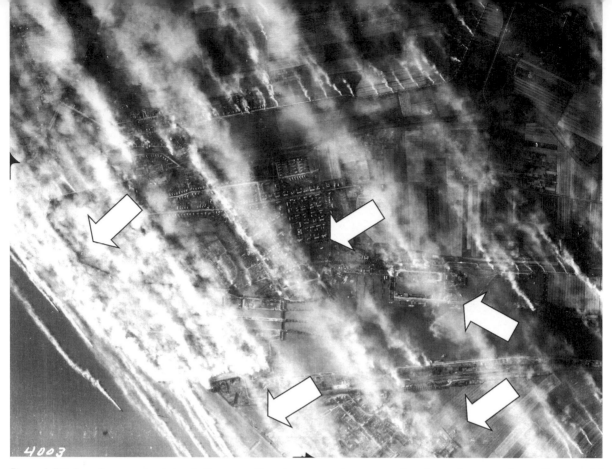

Brunsbüttel under smoke later in the war. Smoke generators were lined up along roads so they could be quickly "lit off" by someone on a bicycle as enemy bombers neared. Under enlargement, I can see several barrage balloons in place (arrows), but all are pulled down to the ground. Heavy bombers flew too high for the balloons to have any effect.

(Below) US 7 Group PR coverage of Bremen, 6 August 1944. An important shipyard and port, but no operational warship would risk being caught here, 35 miles from open water.

KNOW YOUR PORTS—TARANTO

TARANTO, one of the most active of all Italian naval bases, is also an active base for tankers and merchant shipping. Mar Grande, a large enclosed anchorage, has been used regularly by battleships which generally lie within special boom enclosures. A narrow channel through the isthmus on which the town is built connects Mar Grande to the two land locked anchorages of Mar Piccolo. Principal types of naval vessels have been seen in the western part of Mar Piccolo, while the eastern part is used by lighters and small craft. INSET: A smoke screen which was started from the port and town area of TARANTO as U.S.A.A.F. aircraft were on their way to attack Grottaglia Airfield (4.6.43).

MAR PICCOLO (EAST)

MAR PICCOLO (WEST)

TOSI'S SHIPBUILDING YARD

RESTRICTED

Taranto, Italy, was another important port/naval base continually monitored by Allied Intelligence. The inset showing smoke defenses is from 4 June 1943, the base photo mosaic is probably about that time. Both are from an Intelligence publication.

Kiel was one of the most important German naval ports and one of the first targets photographed by the new RAF PR unit using stripped Spitfires flying high and fast to get through Luftwaffe defenses. The crude uncontrolled mosaic (below) was made by the fledgling Photo Interpretation Unit (PIU). This activity is better known as the Central Interpretation Unit (CIU), which it became in January 1941. Lack of earlier coverage kept PIs from realizing the number of ships was unusual—preparations for the Invasion of Norway. The mosaic (which is larger than shown here and mounted on cloth to be folded) shows from the Kiel Canal locks at upper left through various shipyards and drydocks.

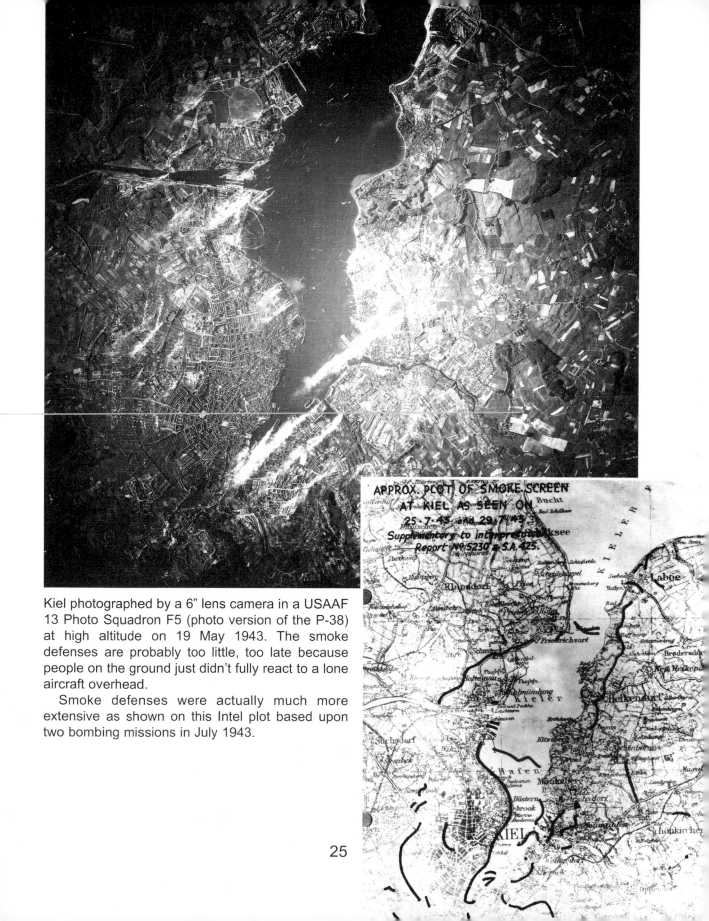

Kiel photographed by a 6" lens camera in a USAAF 13 Photo Squadron F5 (photo version of the P-38) at high altitude on 19 May 1943. The smoke defenses are probably too little, too late because people on the ground just didn't fully react to a lone aircraft overhead.

Smoke defenses were actually much more extensive as shown on this Intel plot based upon two bombing missions in July 1943.

25

(Above) What the smoke looked like during an Eighth Air Force strike on Kiel in May 1943. South is up. The canal is seen snaking off to the upper right.

(Right) Smoke at Kiel in 1944. Note there are even generators on boats. The main shipyards are well covered and it is hard to pick out specific targets. The problem for the Germans was Allied bombers were just area bombing the entire lower port, not necessarily aiming for individual targets so the smoke became irrelevant.

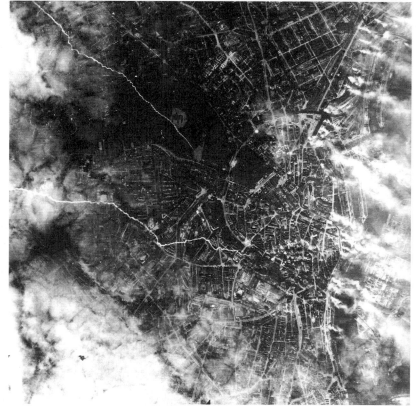

(Above) Kiel on 20 June 1945. Clearly smoke defenses didn't accomplish much. The large capsized hull beside the mole at upper right is Pocket Battleship *Admiral Scheer* (more on that in Chapter III).

Another major port target for the Allies was Hamburg (right), seen under smoke and under attack. The thick billowing smoke at left is from fires. Naval areas are on the right and seem untouched. Hamburg was a place where Schlachtshiffe might be modified or repaired, but didn't have a large anchorage and thus was not a base of naval operations.

27

Hamburg on 6 August 1944. Oil refineries in the port area were the main target and smoke defenses were down. The whitish-gray areas in the city are burned-out blocks mostly destroyed in the "Fire Storms" of July 1943.

My arrow shows one of the war's most famous attempts at camouflage; the fake Lombards Bridge designed to disguise the Aussen Alster, to shift aiming points and protect the heart of the old city.

It didn't work. Below, on 9 April 1943 some of the smoke defense was working at Hamburg, but the wind wasn't blowing the right way. This day's target was U-boat shelters. The inner city is to the right.

Another important port watched closely throughout the war was Stettin (Szczecin), Poland (above). This 540Sq imagery is from 19 February 1944. Even with a naked eye you can see the 861 foot long abandoned hull of carrier *Graf Zeppelin* anchored in the channel at right center leading north to Swinemünde (Swinoujscie) and the Baltic (more in Chapter III).

At the outset of WW II in September 1939, the first German Naval facility the British attempted to recon, then bomb, was the Fleet Anchorage in the Jade Estuary at Wilhelmshaven. It was from there that the German High Seas Fleet had sortied for the Battle of Jutland in 1916, and it was thought that major Kriegsmarine units could be poised to raid sea lanes or challenge the Royal Navy. Both the reconnaissance and bombing were disasters. Half of the 29 bombers failed to find the target and five others were shot down—with no appreciable damage to the German warships attacked.

29

Eighth Air Force B-17s bombing Wilhelmshaven in 1944. Water splashes show "shorts." The lower arrow shows bombs in the air heading for the dock area. The upper arrow points to explosions in the smoke—going after warehouses and oil storage. The wind cooperated so smoke was nicely covering the port, but it didn't matter because of USAAF "formation bombing" (as opposed to individual aircraft trying to bomb a specific point target).

As RAF, and later USAAF, bombing increased, Wilhelmshaven was provided with decoys as passive defenses. RAF photo interpreters at Medmenham quickly spotted them and warned aircrews. Lights, fires and decoys sometimes worked at night (when the RAF bombed), but were almost useless as a defense against daylight bombing.

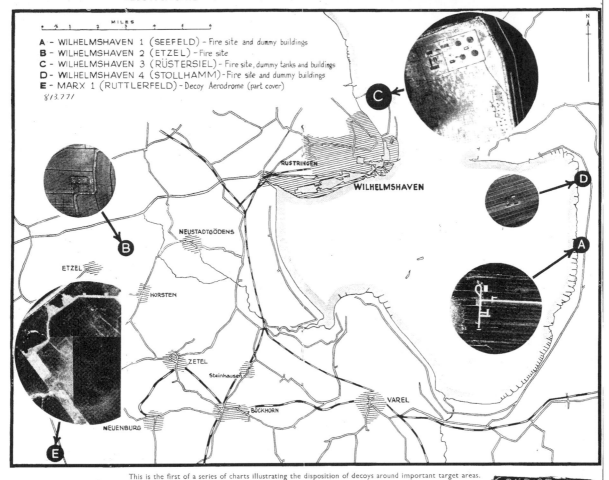

A - WILHELMSHAVEN 1 (SEEFELD) - Fire site and dummy buildings
B - WILHELMSHAVEN 2 (ETZEL) - Fire site
C - WILHELMSHAVEN 3 (RÜSTERSIEL) - Fire site, dummy tanks and buildings
D - WILHELMSHAVEN 4 (STOLLHAMM) - Fire site and dummy buildings
E - MARX 1 (RUTTLERFELD) - Decoy Aerodrome (part cover)

This is the first of a series of charts illustrating the disposition of decoys around important target areas.

Twelve miles northeast of Gdynia and fifteen miles north of Danzig, Helle was a natural anchorage for warships staging out of either port or working up in the Baltic (see left map at start of this chapter for location). Photos in following chapters will show heavy ships here. The resolution of this 3 August 1944 imagery isn't sufficient to identify the two ships just off shore, but shapes, rough scaling using the known size of the breakwater, and what we know about warships frequenting Gdynia and Danzig in this time period, suggest a cruiser closest to the land and a pocket battleship in deeper water.

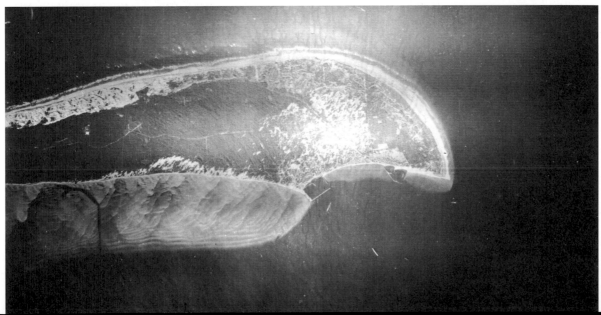

Before demands of the invasion of Russia and operations in North Africa the Luftwaffe was strongest in Western Europe and the Kriegsmarine risked putting major surface units in occupied Atlantic ports that were well within range of the RAF. Luftwaffe fighters forced British aircraft to attack at night into the teeth of dense anti-aircraft artillery defenses.

(Below) Brest, France in 1940, possibly from a bomber. It is easy to see how confusing and difficult bomb aiming would be under those conditions (searchlights, tracers, flares, fires, flak bursts). Little Intelligence beyond ship ID could be gleaned from such imagery. Without the "gouge," or adjoining photos, it is difficult to plot or decipher the photo. Night photography is a time exposure so the thin lines are lights the plane is moving over. Wide lines are from flares dropped to illuminate the scene for photography. Annotation "2" may be searchlights, and the fuel storage tank farm just below the upper "2" is recognizable.

Brest was well masked by smoke during a 16 April 1943 Eighth Air Force strike. Earlier RAF attacks had been on port facilities and German surface ships. USAAF attacks were on sub-pens. An operations note on this mission said that "air defense was intense." A few of the better defined black blobs are flak bursts, most are imperfections in the neg.

I can't leave this cursory review of ports without showing an example of the subtleties and oddities seen on aerial imagery that can reveal a broader status or condition on the ground. Density of shipping and apparent movement—ships coming and going, associated rail traffic, changes in defenses and obvious work being done.

(Below) An enlargement of 2 September 1944 RAF coverage of Gdynia's outer harbor shows what is probably pre-*Dreadnought* Battleship SMS *Schleswig-Holstein*. During a "courtesy call" on Danzig, at 0445 hours on 1 September 1939, this German training ship began firing its 11" and 6.7 " guns on Polish forts, starting the German Invasion of Poland…and ultimately World War II.

Coverage of 24 March 1945, (above), shows what is certainly *Schleswig-Holstein* moved to the inner harbor to have its 11" turrets and guns pulled out, presumably to use in fixed defense positions against the advancing Soviets (barbettes appear as holes). The other old BB usually seen in Gdynia, SMS *Schlesien*, was reported shelling Soviet troops near Danzig in March, so this can't be him.[1] The mole shows newly earth-revetted buildings, fox holes and at least three bomb craters. Records say RAF bombing sank the ship in shallow water on the 18th. Perhaps this counts as sunk? A broader look at the Inner Harbor (see the ninth photo in this chapter) shows this as one of the few ships left in the port—sure signs that the end of the war was nearing rapidly and desperate measures were the order of the day.

Unlike the British, American and Japanese Navies, with the exception of submarines, ships of the German, French and Italian navies weren't expected to spend long periods at sea so Allied Intelligence focused on European ports to keep track of them. Initially they looked at places where the heavy ships were built: Kiel, Wilhelmshaven and Hamburg. Later it was the main ports and Naval Bases: Kiel, Gdynia, Toulon, Oran, Taranto and La Spezia. Threat of aerial attack pushed some German ships east along the Baltic coast as far as harbors in East Prussia. After the German occupation of France, Atlantic ports with facilities for large ships (St. Nazaire and Brest), also became places for Intelligence to watch for German warships. By 1942 that focus became for a watch for U-boats and E-boats.

Kiel had a large anchorage and was far enough from England to be relatively safe from air attacks early in the war. German naval units based at Kiel could sortie into the Baltic, into the North Atlantic via one of three Danish straits, or into the North Sea after transiting the Kiel Canal to Brunsbüttel and the Elbe Estuary.

As World War II developed into an air-land war in Europe and a submarine war in the Atlantic, Axis surface raiders became less likely and less relevant—and so did their lairs.

FOOTNOTE

[1]Though it feels awkward, my text will honor the Kriegsmarine (War Navy) tradition by referring to warships as masculine.

CHAPTER III
KRIEGSMARINE

The German Navy had three classes of warships larger than cruisers: battleships, what are more properly battlecruisers, and the so called pocket battleships, but these totaled just seven vessels in 1940. Stripped of warships after World War I, Germany wasn't able to create enough surface ships to face the formidable Royal Navy as they had at Jutland. In that battle, with a much larger force, Germany had only tried to carve off and destroy a portion of the British navy. Ship vs. ship they might have been superior, but in 1939 no one in Germany thought their seven big ships were a heavy surface force on a par with even the French Navy. The most naïve or zealous Nazi official would have been deemed mad to pit the Kriegsmarine in an all-out toe-to-toe fight against the seventy-plus battleships, battlecruisers and heavy cruisers of the Royal Navy—there would be no Second Jutland in the 1940s.

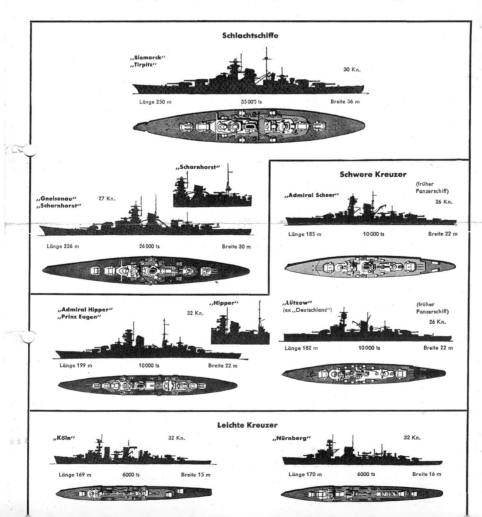

No one in Germany thought that situation would be reversed in time to affect what was expected to be a short war—it took years to design, build and work-up a major warship. They expected the war would be over quickly and naval actions would be confined to commerce raiding and support to ground offensives, such as the invasion of Norway.

It is impossible to consider the resources and effort expended making those seven major ships and not speculate that one reason for the existence of those large warships was national pride. There was also a specific purpose for them; a limited objective. They were intended to disrupt Britain's ocean lifelines and stretch the Royal Navy in wild-goose chases, counting on the speed and gun-power of Germany's new ships to win over any equal number of enemy warships. Commerce raiding had been a successful tactic during WW I but by 1940 was overtaken by surveillance and detection technology. In retrospect, the men and material sunk into those seven large surface warships would have had more results on the intended interdiction mission if expended on submarines.

However, alone or in combination those seven heavy ships could be devastating commerce raiders in the Atlantic, disrupting, even severing, Britain's life lines from North America and the Commonwealth in Africa and Asia. Many of the Royal Navy's heavy warships were of WW I-era construction while the German ships had all the latest design, materials and technology. Their speed and firepower made it easy to run down and capture or sink helpless merchantmen typically alone or guarded by destroyers with good speed but only 4" guns or smaller. Given their speed, it was thought (assumed/hoped) the German commerce raiders could evade or avoid engagement with more heavily-gunned vessels. Successful forays into open waters early in the war seemed to confirm the surface-raider role. However, Allied Signals Intelligence, radar, long-range aerial reconnaissance and aerial attack made the surface commerce raider concept a suicide mission after 1941.

For much of the rest of WW II surviving German heavy warships lurked in sheltered, defended locations, poised to launch out at convoys, tying down many times their numbers of Allied warships simply by being a threat. With ships such as *Tirpitz* in a fjord near the northern tip of Norway, Allied convoys bound for the Soviet Union were driven north into colder, more dangerous Arctic waters and farther from Allied air support. The Allies were forced to allocate large warships to defensive/intercept positions—making them unavailable to support convoys, assault landings and other military operations on sea or land.

POCKET BATTLESHIPS

Laid down in the early 1930s and all operational before the war, the Germans referred to the pocket battleships as Panzershiffe (armored ships). In February 1940 they were officially reclassified as Schwere Kreuzers (Heavy Cruisers). Their relatively light weight was intended to avoid exceeding pre-war Versailles Treaty limits.

(Below) *Graf Spee* photographed at Hamburg before the war, probably from an "open source."

I believe pocket battleships were a brilliant fit with the obsolescent commerce raider concept. They were well designed and unique in WW II, built to out-gun cruisers and out-run ships with heavier armament. Welded construction rather than riveted gave more ship for the weight. At 10,000 tons *Deutschland, Admiral Scheer* and *Admiral Graf Spee* were equal to heavy cruisers in weight and

speed but their six 11" main batteries in two large armored turrets (again to save weight) outranged the 8" guns on heavy cruisers in other navies. Similar to heavy cruisers in shape and beam, and with length between light and heavy cruisers, the unusually large turrets fore and aft made the pocket battleships relatively easy to identify even on small scale aerial photos. *Deutschland* was renamed *Lützow* in November 1939 because Hitler didn't want to risk loss of a ship named "Germany."

Straight bow *Graf Spee* had only been commissioned a little more than a year when he joined the 1937 Spithead Review. HMS *Resolution* and *Hood* are in the background.

Before the war, before ship-hunting techniques were tested and perfected, the pocket battleships were much feared as lone, fast, commerce raiders ranging free in the Atlantic. But the Allies also knew the weaknesses of those ships. Lack of armor and weight of volley fire put them at a disadvantage in a fight with other major warships. The pocket battleships used diesel engines, so they suffered from limited range. Loose in the Atlantic they needed consorts to refuel and resupply them. Since the support ships were essentially merchant vessels with low speed, they could not accompany the warships. Rendezvous had to be arranged, and that required radio transmissions that could be intercepted or result in Direction Finding triangulation to give away the location of either ship. Supply ships were vulnerable to sinking or capture by much faster enemy cruisers and destroyers. The Allies knew once vital support was cut off, the pocket battleships would soon be stranded or prey cornered by a force with heavier guns. But knowing all that was not the same as doing it. The oceans are vast. Commerce raider's supply ships were adept at flying neutral flags, changing their silhouette, shunning regular sea lanes and maintaining radio discipline.

All three pocket battleships had productive cruises early in the war, mainly beyond the reach of British Intelligence collection capability of the time. Built at Wilhelmshaven and commissioned in January 1936; *Graf Spee* was the newest of the class, and many thought the best, so he was first to sortie for war, going to sea from Wilhelmshaven on 21 August 1939 (ten days before war began). *Spee* was sent to the South Atlantic as a commerce raider in waters seldom frequented by the Royal Navy and far beyond the reach of British aerial reconnaissance.

At that time the RAF couldn't reliably get aerial photos of German ports and pre-war ground intelligence on warship locations was sketchy. Radio transmissions may have disclosed that *Spee* was "out" and DF of transmissions could roughly follow his progress. Of course those sources grew increasingly "cold" with time and distance from shore-based intercept stations. From 30 September on, the most reliable locational information was brief distress signals from Allied ships *Spee* was engaging. Unlike the later no-holds-barred submarine war, *Spee* engaged in a gentleman's war, using speed and combat power to overhaul and stop nine merchant ships, board them, and put the crew off safely before sinking their ships. The 303 captured sailors were held in *Spee*'s tanker/supply ship *Altmark* and later freed off Norway by a Royal Navy destroyer.

37

From sightings, radio direction finding and reports of sinkings, the Royal Navy knew generally where the pocket battleship was, but their knowledge was always a day or two behind. The fast warship was cruising back and forth in search of easy pickings. Nine British Battle Groups of battleships, battlecruisers, aircraft carriers, light and heavy cruisers were rushed into the South Atlantic and Indian Ocean to hunt down the nettling German raider. On 13 December, *Spee* was finally sighted and engaged by 8" gun cruiser HMS *Exeter*, and 6" cruisers HMS *Ajax* and HMNZS *Achilles*. Here was the encounter for which *Spee* had been built. The British ships had a slight speed advantage and hundreds of years of tradition behind them. They refused to be driven off by *Spee*'s heavier guns, attacking repeatedly, damaging the German warship and forcing it to port in neutral Montevideo, Uruguay for repairs. British agents viewing the ship reported 60 hits had taken out some secondary batteries and, more important, *Spee*'s rangefinders. Hague Convention Treaty regulations allowed the warship to remain in safety and without internment for 24 hours, but it also had to give belligerent merchant ships a 24 hour head start before leaving the port. The British Consul arranged to have British ships trickle out of Montevideo on a schedule that bottled *Spee* up while he lobbied for internment of the ship and crew. The delay also gave time for heavy ships of the Royal Navy to converge on the waters off Uruguay.

The German captain knew he was trapped, short of fuel and with the accuracy of his main weapons diminished. British Intelligence planted stories convincing Captain Langsdorff that he was likely out-gunned if he left port. Actually *Exeter* was too seriously damaged to take part in a battle and only 6" cruisers *Ajax*, *Achilles* and newly arrived 8" cruiser *Cumberland* were waiting to face *Spee*. Wanting to save the surviving crew and avoid a clear-cut defeat at the hands of the Royal Navy, pocket Battleship *Admiral Graf Spee* was scuttled in shallow water just beyond the port on 17 December 1939. He's still there.

Class leader for the three pocket battleships, *Deutschland* was built at Kiel, commissioned in April 1933, and based at Kiel. Renamed *Lützow*, this ship was well known to British Intelligence. He'd been off Spain several times during the Spanish Civil War but for most of WW II remained in port or in the Baltic. After repair of damage from shore batteries during the Invasion of Norway, *Lützow*'s North Atlantic sortie was aborted when he was torpedoed by a British submarine north of Denmark.

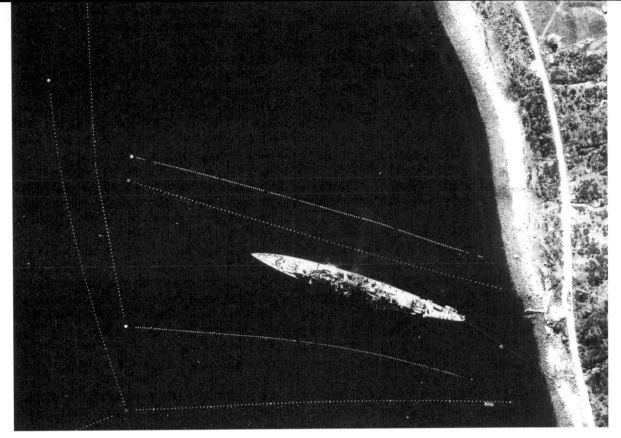

In June 1941 the ship was hit again by an RAF torpedo plane and back in Kiel for repairs. *Lützow* was involved in several minor engagements in the far North Atlantic from December 1941 on but achieved little.

The characteristic large three-gun turrets fore and aft unmistakably identify *Lützow* in Bogen fjord, 11 June 1942. Those lines of "beads" in the water are floats holding up anti-torpedo nets protecting the pocket battleship.

(Below) *Lützow* off Norway, 16 May 1942. This 1PRU photo looks like someone was trying to bomb the ship—albeit not very well.

Lützow's major war contribution was as a floating artillery battery supporting ground forces in the Baltic. RAF bombs sent him to the bottom in shallow water off Swinemünde in April 1945. He was raised but scuttled on 4 May 1945 as Russian forces advanced on land. Raised by the Soviets after the war, *Lützow* was used as a target ship until 1949.

Schwerer Kreuzer (Panzerschiff) **„Admiral Scheer".** *10 000 t.*

Admiral Scheer was the most active and most successful vessel of this class.

Built at Wilhelmshaven, he was commissioned in November 1934 and went into refit in early 1940 for superstructure modernization and getting the forward raked "Atlantic bow" found advantageous in the open ocean. From 27 October 1940 to 1 April 1941, he raided from the North Atlantic to the south and around the tip of Africa to waters north of Madagascar, tying up large numbers of Allied ships and aircraft to find him.

Admiral Scheer at Swinemünde, 22 April 1943.

Returning in triumph to Kiel following the longest and most successful commerce raiding sortie of the war, *Scheer* didn't leave port again for more than a year, then served in the Arctic with minor success before going back to Kiel.

Out again in late 1944 in support of retreating Germany forces in the Baltic, the ship was finally worn out. Below, extreme enlargement of *Scheer* off Swinemünde in January 1944.

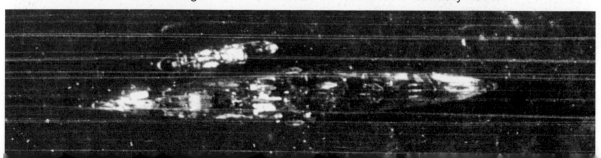

Scheer and *Lützow* together at Gdynia in late 1944. They were working in the Baltic supporting retreating German ground forces. Shadows show the left ship with an original straight bow configuration, identifying *Lützow*, and a clipper bow on *Scheer* at the right.

Two more late-war looks at *Scheer*. (Above) 27 August 1944 at Gdynia. Below, off Helle on 25 March 1945. The eight 5.9" secondary batteries and quadruple tube torpedo launchers aft were being exercised.

Scheer went to Kiel for much needed work. (Above) is 22 March 1945 the large turrets and two torpedo launchers show well. On 9 April 1945 he was hit by RAF heavy bombers and capsized in this location (compare position with the June 1945 imagery of Kiel in Chapter II).

The photo (below) was taken shortly after Allied forces entered Kiel (probably June 1945).

BATTLECRUISERS

Sometimes referred to as the "ugly sisters," to my eyes, the two ships in this class, *Gneisenau* and *Scharnhorst*, were among the prettiest ships of the war. Their good looks were improved when clipper bows were installed just before the war to make them more seaworthy in the open Atlantic. At 226 meters long and at just under 40,000 tons (loaded), they were armored like battleships and could reach 33 knots. Their main drawback was being under-gunned with main batteries of nine 11" guns. That made them formidable against anything up to heavy cruisers but at a serious disadvantage against battleships mounting 14" to 16" guns, (most of which the "sisters" could easily outrun).

The "sisters" were conceptually the mirror image of pocket battleships. They were well-armored but under-gunned where the pocket battleships were heavily-gunned for their size but under-armored. It was as though the Kriegsmarine was searching for the winning mix, but the day of the battlecruiser had passed.

(Below) *Scharnhorst* at Kiel in October 1939, manning the side to honor Günter Prien and his *U-47* (a Type VIIB submarine) returning from a daring raid on the Royal Navy anchorage of Scapa Flow where the U-boat sank Battleship HMS *Royal Oak*.

Both battlecruisers were laid down in the spring of 1935, *Scharnhorst* at Wilhelmshaven and *Gneisenau* at Kiel. *Gneisenau* finished first, and was commissioned in May 1938 under the watchful eyes of British Naval Attachés and agents. *Scharnhorst* was commissioned in January 1939. The twins were out in the Atlantic and North Sea twice in 1939, off Norway again in May and June 1940.

The two battlecruisers were usually at sea together and early in the war were among the most active of German surface ships—and most effective when cost and effort are weighed against results. Like a pair of big cats hunting, the battlecruisers working together sank carrier HMS *Glorious* and two accompanying destroyers.

Scharnhorst took a torpedo hit during the attack on *Glorious* and had to drydock at Kiel. The pair was out in the Atlantic again from January to March 1941, sinking 22 merchant ships between them as they ranged as far south as the Equator, successfully eluding Royal Navy reconnaissance and pursuing surface forces.

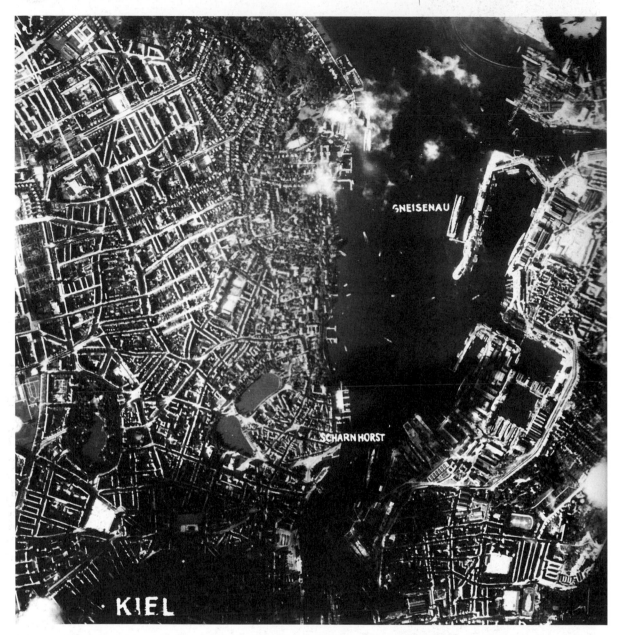

GNEISENAU

SCHARNHORST

KIEL

A PRU Spitfire photographed both battlecruisers in drydock at Kiel, 1 August 1940. Aerial imagery with this scale and resolution was suitable for ship identification but little Intelligence about status, capabilities or intentions could result, still it was important to know where the warships were on any given day.

Drydocks to the right of *Scharnhorst* hold a heavy cruiser and light cruiser. Another heavy cruiser is moored against the quay to the right of *Gneisenau*. These ships were all probably repairing and refurbishing after wear and damage incurred during the German Invasion of Norway.

Kiel in 1940. As near as I can tell; "A" has off-set rear turrets making it K-class Light Cruiser *Köln* (*Königsberg* and *Karlsruhe* were sunk by this time). "B" is heavy cruiser, probably *Hipper*. "C" is the Krupp Submarine Yards with several submarines in drydock beside it. "D" is *Gneisenau* in a floating drydock. "E" is a Pocket Battleship, probably *Lützow*, in drydock. "F" indicates Motor Torpedo Boats and "G" are coastal/Baltic submarines—based upon size and location, probably training boats.

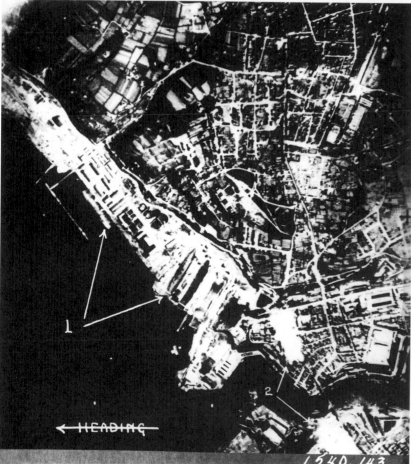

Gneisenau from Scharnhorst in June 1940, on the North Atlantic sortie during which they sank carrier HMS Glorious.

Returning from their most successful sortie, the ships went to Brest which proved to be a bad choice since it turned out the Luftwaffe couldn't protect them.

At Brest they were particularly vulnerable at night, and the RAF really wanted to destroy those ships. The "ugly sisters" were attacked several times by bombers from England, sustaining enough damage each time to require more repairs to make them seaworthy.

BREST.
Taken by 58 Squadron. Date 5.5.41.
Time 0120 hours. Height 13,000 ft. Simplified Camera.
(1) Battle cruisers "Scharnhorst" and "Gneisenau" (Netting Camouflage). (2) Smoke originating from fires started during the attack.
No bomb flashes or burst recorded.

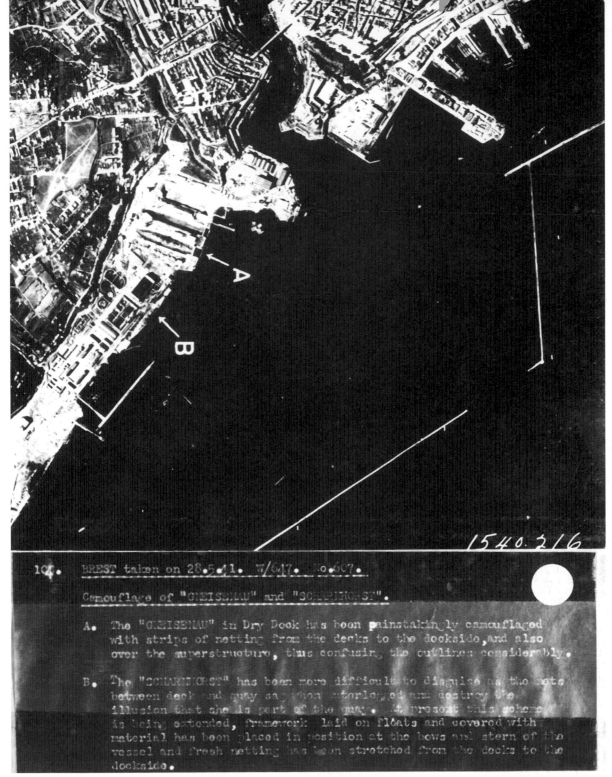

104. BREST taken on 28.5.41. W/647. No.607.

Camouflage of "GNEISENAU" and "SCHARNHORST".

A. The "GNEISENAU" in Dry Dock has been painstakingly camouflaged with strips of netting from the decks to the dockside, and also over the superstructure, thus confusing the outlines considerably.

B. The "SCHARNHORST" has been more difficult to disguise as the nets between deck and quay say have interlocked and destroy the illusion that she is part of the quay. At present this scheme is being extended, framework laid on floats and covered with material has been placed in position at the bows and stern of the vessel and fresh netting has been stretched from the decks to the dockside.

With two major warships just 120 miles south of Plymouth, the RAF tried to get PR cover every few days and bomb them frequently at night when the Luftwaffe couldn't interfere.

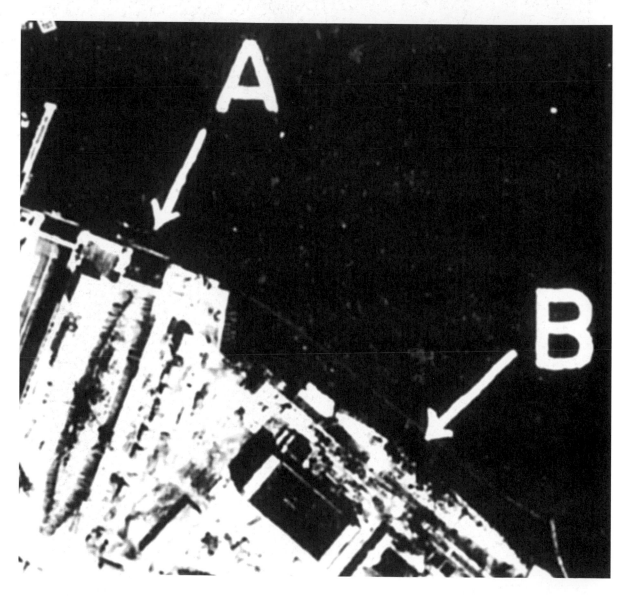

The big ships were frequently alongside quays but just as often in one of the drydocks for repair of minor damage. The longer they remained at Brest the more vulnerable they became. As long as minor damage from air attacks was tying them to Brest's repair facilities the "sisters" were not able to sortie as raiders—making them a liability rather than asset. This enlargement of the photo above shows extensive netting used to disguise *Gneisenau* in drydock and floats put fore and aft on *Scharnhorst* to confuse its shape—pretty much a waste of time and effort since the drydock and ship locations were well known to the RAF.

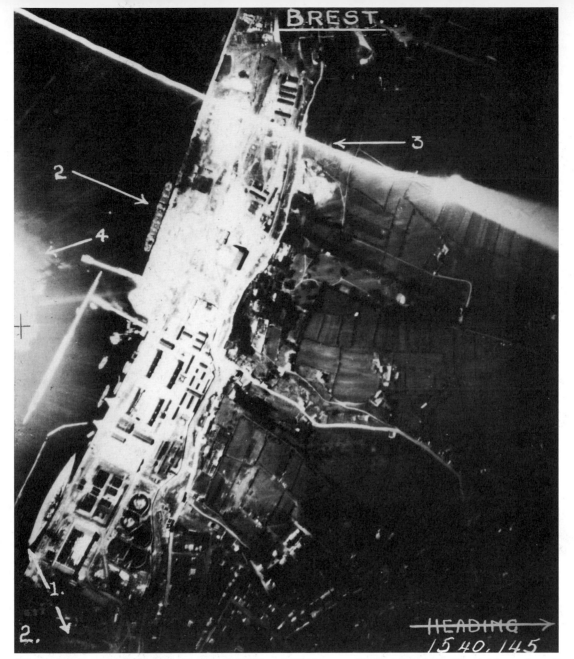

(Above) Brest photographed by RAF 149Sq, 2205 hours, 30 March 1941. The taking aircraft was at 8,500 feet. *Scharnhorst* is beside the quay and *Gneisenau* in drydock (annotation "1"). "2" is a large tanker. "3" a searchlight and "4" appears to be a "lens flare" from the night photography. The graceful hull-lines of the battlecruiser are unmistakable. Imagery like this was mainly taken to make sure the ships were still in port.

By December it was clear that their potential threat to Atlantic convoys didn't overbalance their vulnerability at Brest. On 11-13 February 1942, the two battlecruisers and heavy cruiser *Prinz Eugen* humiliated and infuriated the entire British war machine in Operation Cerberus (well known as the Channel Dash) by boldly sailing from Brest, right up the English Channel to German home waters in the face of everything the Royal Navy, RAF and coastal artillery batteries could cobble together on short notice.

Gneisenau hit a mine off the Netherlands during the "Channel Dash" and went to Kiel for hull repair. RAF attacks on *Gneisenau* in drydock on 26 and 27 February 1942 started a fire that exploded stored munitions, blowing off his bow. A short temporary bow was fabricated and the battlecruiser sailed to Gdynia for decommissioning and a major overhaul.

Above is 540Sq. imagery of both battlecruisers on 20 August 1942. The upper arrow is *Scharnhorst* and an almost unrecognizable *Gneisenau* is the lower.

RAF photoreconnaissance of Gdynia watched the damaged BC on a regular basis.[1]

Enlargement of 1 August 1942 imagery shows *Gneisenau*'s short temporary bow still in place but the guns and turrets have been pulled and you can see down into the barbettes. A shadow shows the large floating crane at upper right. It may have been moved to that location for heavy work on the battlecruiser.

By 12 December 1942 the temporary bow had been removed. There is post-war evidence that there was some thought of reconditioning *Gneisenau* and rearming with 15" main batteries, making a truly formidable warship. But that turned out to be just another German scattering of scarce resources on questionable projects with doubtful ends.

51

On 20 August 1942 *Scharnhorst* was in the "ready to sortie" position in Gdynia's outer harbor.

(Right) A German photo caught an ice-coated *Scharnhorst* active in Arctic waters, threatening convoys to Soviet ports.

(Below) Enlargement of *Scharnhorst* maneuvering at speed off Norway, 12 December 1942.

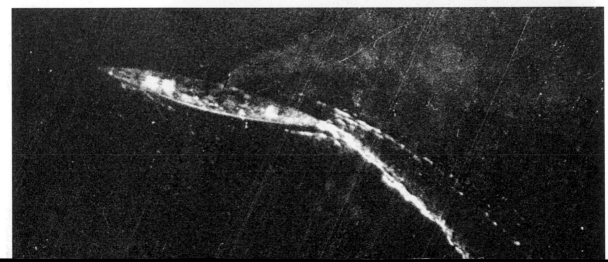

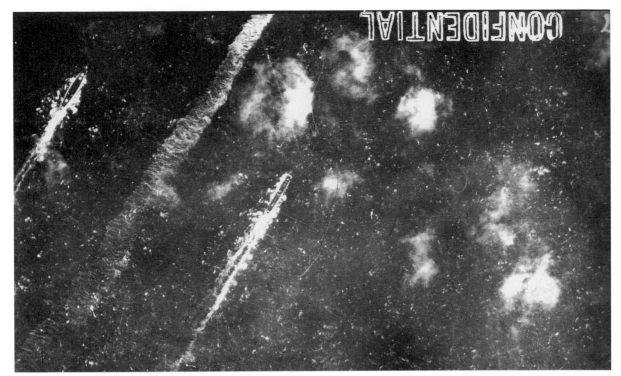

On 25 January 1943 540Sq. caught German warships at speed off Norway. *Scharnhorst* is at upper left—the three turrets show plainly. I wish I had the next photo in the series because the larger wake disappearing off the frame is probably *Tirpitz*.

Daring agents in Norway photographed and smuggled out evidence of German ships in Kaafjord on 15 August 1943. Annotations say number "1" is the old Norwegian ship *Tordenskjord* (probably actually the coastal defense ship *Tordenskjold*). "2" is *Lützow*. "3 and 4" are destroyers. "5" indicates torpedo nets. "6" is *Scharnhorst*.

A Norwegian agent caught *Scharnhorst* entering Kaafjord at 0330 hours on 5 August 1943. Note lengths of the bow and stern camouflage-painted light gray in an attempt to make the ship appear shorter and confuse enemy identification/optical ranging.

Scharnhorst and consorts in a Norwegian fjord, 23 September 1943.

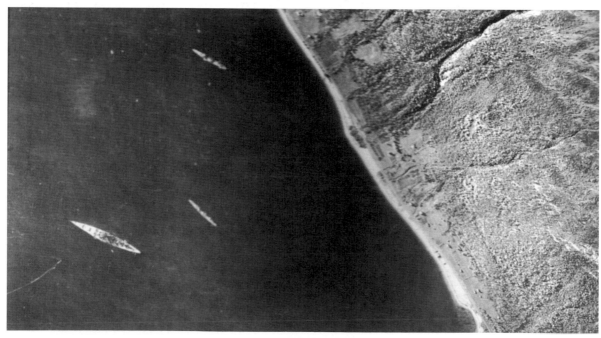

Meanwhile, back at Gdynia on 10 October 1943, *Gneisenau* had wooden sheds built over the three barbettes and false work "reshaping" the stern. It looks like netting has been draped over the superstructure in a futile attempt to disguise the ship. To the left are Light Cruiser *Leipzig*, and the bow of another light cruiser, by default, *Nürnberg*. On the opposite side of the mole is old Battleship SMS *Schleswig-Holstein* in front of five submarines of two distinct classes. The large floating crane (lower left of the above photo) has been moved well away from the battlecruiser, suggesting heavy work on that vessel is suspended.

On 2 September 1944 something was definitely going on with *Gneisenau's* turrets, the wooden roofs had been removed and there were materials on deck nearby. Light Cruiser *Emden* is in front of the battlecruiser. The ship showing crosses on its deck is former SMS Battleship *Hessen*, converted to a radio-controlled target ship in the 1930s. Mooring the essentially idle vessels outboard of the battlecruiser suggests its own status at the time. Therefore the activity may be more dismantling.

(Above) 12 August 1944 saw an upswing in activity in the port, possibly because warships were now being used farther east firing in direct support of retreating German soldiers and Gdynia was a good base of operations. It appears that some work has begun again on *Gneisenau*. Alongside is SMS *Zähringen*, another old battleship converted to a radio-controlled target ship in the 1930s. Farther left is *Lützow*. Across the mole is Light Cruiser *Nurenberg*. *Hessen* is moved closer to the channel (and has an outbound U-boat beside him). Top center is what many considered the Kriegsmarine's luckiest ship, the elegant Heavy Cruiser *Prinz Eugen*.

Yard work continued until December 1943, when sister ship *Scharnhorst* was sunk off the north tip of Norway during attack on a convoy. The battlecruiser's vulnerabilities were now apparent, and convoys to England and the Soviet Union were being escorted by Allied battleships and small aircraft carriers. An up-gunned battlecruiser would have been a formidable companion for *Tirpitz* and *Scharnhorst* in 1943, but heavier Allied firepower defending potential objectives made *Gneisenau*'s upgrade a dead-end not worth the expenditure of scarce resources in 1944. By late 1944, work had ceased on the stricken BC.

As Soviet Armies approached, the battlecruiser was sunk as a block ship in the Gdynia channel on 27 March 1945. Above is *Gneisenau* on 24 March 1945, in the "ready to sortie" position beside the channel of the Outer Harbor, stern toward the Baltic.

TRUE BATTLESHIPS

When commissioned in August 1940, at 50,000 tons and 823.5 feet long, *Bismarck* was thought to be the largest, most powerful battleship afloat, flouting the post-World War I Naval Treaties and the Surrender restrictions. Actually the Japanese *Yamato*, launched in the same month, was 26,000 tons heavier and mounted nine 18" naval rifles, but Allied Intelligence knew nothing about that little surprise until later in the war.

Bismarck was an impressive ship by any standard; fast, powerful, well-armored, with state-of-the-art radar fire-control—but he was alone.

Naturally *Bismarck* was one of the first British PR objectives of the war. He had been in the water for fifteen months, but wasn't yet operational when first imaged at Hamburg's Blohm und Voss Yards on 18 May 1940, below. The imagery scale only allowed for identification.

Laid down at Hamburg before the war, *Bismarck* was known to Allied Intelligence, but only in the early stages of building. Thirty knot speed and eight of the latest design 15" naval rifles made him a formidable weapon. British Intel wanted to know where he was, what he was doing and what he could do.

Regular aerial photoreconnaissance of Hamburg watched *Bismarck*'s progress to full operation.

(Right) *Bismarck* fitting out in the Blohm und Voss Yards on 11 September 1940. Again, this imagery permitted identification but allowed for no interpretation of details.

Below, a 14 October 1940 photo was thought to indicate "tweaking" back at the builder's yard at Hamburg following a short trial sortie.

The battleship was next seen at Kiel just beyond the Kiel Canal locks (at left). Early March 1940. The open Baltic was just up and to the right.

(Below) Kiel on 12 March 1941.

Bismarck was in a floating drydock for adjustments after a shakedown cruise in the Baltic. Light Cruiser *Leipzig*, is in the drydock just to the right and two drydocks farther up are four submarines (seen as two pairs) in work. The other annotation (upper right) is one of the Pocket Battleships, probably *Hipper*.

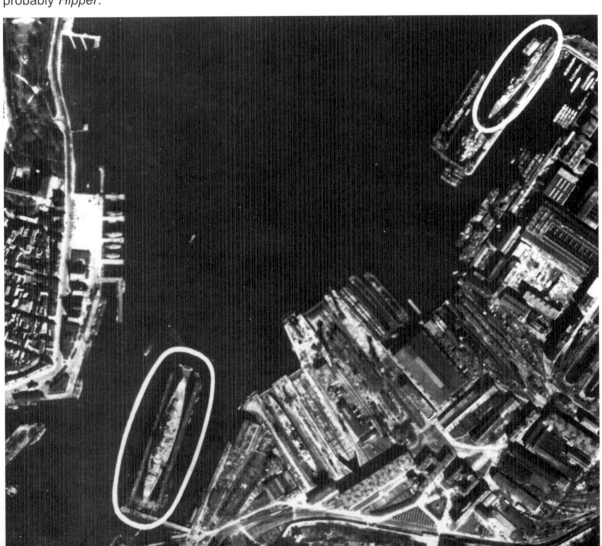

It was expected that the new battleship was faster and more powerful than all but a few Royal Navy battleships,[2] meaning with good handling, good Intelligence and good luck the German ship could likely engage the Royal Navy on his own terms. Unfortunately *Bismarck* didn't have much of those latter three. British Intelligence fully expected the ship would be used as a commerce raider like the pocket battleships and battlecruisers—and be much harder to stop. They watched it carefully during fitting out and four months of shake-down in the Baltic, trying to determine when and how he would enter the war.

British Intelligence only lost sight of *Bismarck* for a few days during the ship's total operational life of nine months, following the BB from Hamburg to Gdyna, Poland and into the Atlantic. After the Baltic work-up, *Bismarck*, in the company of Heavy Cruiser *Prinz Eugen*, left Gdynia on 19 May 1941, heading west. The warships and eleven accompanying destroyers (anti-submarine screen) and freighters (supply and support vessels) were spotted by a British informative in Sweden as they transited the Kattegat on 20 May. Signals Intelligence had provided indications of the battleship breaking out into the Atlantic, so no one was surprised. The Royal Navy had to find the battleship again quickly and destroy it.

Searching the Norwegian Coast on 21 May 1941, a photorecon Spitfire located the target battleship in Dobric Fjord near Bergen (about the same latitude as the Shetlands).

The RAF caption on this photo read, "The BISMARCK in an isolated fjord not far from BERGEN. This shows supply ships arriving to re-victual and re-fuel the BISMARCK just before she left on her raiding expedition." Consort Heavy Cruiser *Prinz Eugen* was in another fjord five miles south of Bergen. Presence of a tanker and absence of torpedo nets told British PIs the BB didn't plan to remain here long.

60

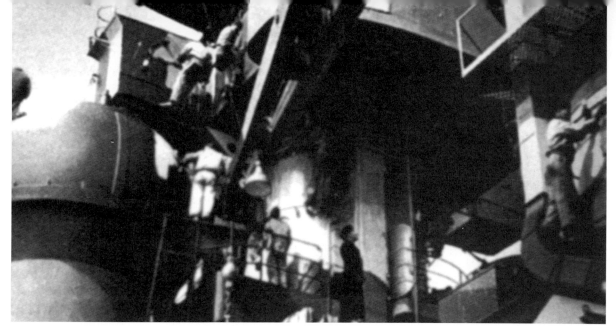

Taken at 1300 hours, just two hours after the battleship entered the fjord, the imagery had to get back to England, be processed and interpreted. All that took time. As supplies were being transferred, the German crew painted the ship with new "disruptive" camouflage.

Seen from *Eugen*, the new paint job was necessarily simple because of the time available, but it did feature darkening of the bow and stern intended to disguise the length of the ship (this was the reverse of the light-dark coloring seen on *Scharnhorst* earlier).

Some sources show drawings of *Bismarck* with large swastikas on black bands on the deck fore and aft. An enlargement of the last time the RAF saw the ship from above shows that, unless those Nazi markings were added after 21 May, they weren't present during his fateful sortie.

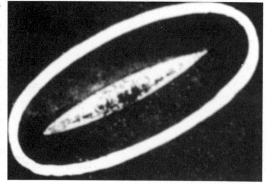

61

A quickly dispatched RAF bombing raid was too late. *Bismarck* and *Eugen* had sailed on the 23rd and were loose in the North Atlantic.

(Left) *Bismarck* with his darkened bow as seen from *Prinz Eugen*.

The sortie was supposed to include *Tirpitz* but he wasn't ready so the two new battlewagons headed northwest alone, circling north of Iceland to slip past British warships from Scapa Flow

giving chase. The opposing forces met in the Denmark Strait, west of Iceland on 24 May.

(Below and Right) Two photos taken from *Prinz Eugen* show *Bismarck* firing on HMS *Hood* and new BB HMS *Prince of Wales*.

Ten minutes after the engagement began a lucky round penetrated *Hood*'s lightly armored deck and exploded the battlecruiser's aft magazine.

HMS *Hood* went down with all but three of her crew. Battleship *Prince of Wales* broke off the

fight a short time later and *Bismarck* headed southwest into the open Atlantic with minor damage, and shadowed by British Heavy Cruisers *Norfolk* (right) and *Suffolk*.

(Below) A Consolidated "Catalina" PBY patrol plane. Once spotted it's hard to stop position

reports from an aircraft with 2,500 mile range that is staying beyond your guns.

The German warships were now prey to two new elements in sea warfare: radar and aerial reconnaissance. They knew they probably couldn't shake free. Position report updates meant more elements of the Royal Navy would be converging at flank speed from the north and south.

62

(Right) A Royal Navy "County Cruiser" with HMS *Prince of Wales* in the distance during the hunt for *Bismarck*. 24 May 1940.

Knowing pursuit would concentrate on *Bismarck*, *Eugen* was cut loose to head south, deeper into the Atlantic, while the damaged battleship headed east toward Saint Nazaire, France and the only drydock on the Atlantic coast large enough to hold it. Slowed by further damaged from aerial torpedoes and unable to properly steer, *Bismarck* was finally caught well short of the French coast and Luftwaffe fighter cover. Converging Royal Navy surface and air units sank the battleship on the morning of 27 May 1941, nine days after he began his first combat sortie.

One of the last photos of *Bismarck* shows an erratic course cause by steering with engines. If not for a torpedo from an *Ark Royal* "Swordfish" bi-plane jamming his rudder, *Bismarck* could probably have out-run the slower British ships to St Nazaire and relative safety.

Circling far south Prinz Eugen refueled from a pre-positioned supply ship. Running at best speed the cruiser successfully reached Brest on 1 June.

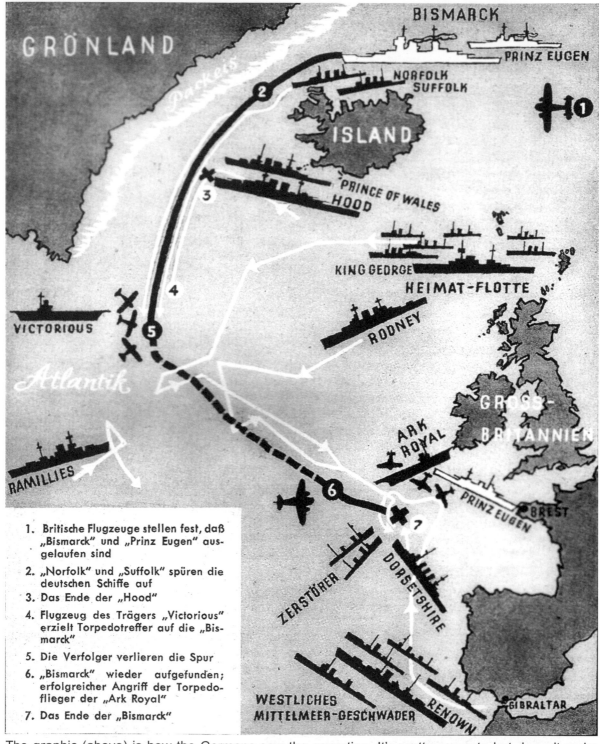

GRÖNLAND

BISMARCK

PRINZ EUGEN

NORFOLK
SUFFOLK

ISLAND

PRINCE OF WALES
HOOD

KING GEORGE

HEIMAT-FLOTTE

RODNEY

VICTORIOUS

Atlantik

GROSS-
BRITANNIEN

ARK
ROYAL

RAMILLIES

PRINZ EUGEN

BREST

ZERSTÖRER

DORSETSHIRE

1. Britische Flugzeuge stellen fest, daß „Bismarck" und „Prinz Eugen" ausgelaufen sind

2. „Norfolk" und „Suffolk" spüren die deutschen Schiffe auf

3. Das Ende der „Hood"

4. Flugzeug des Trägers „Victorious" erzielt Torpedotreffer auf die „Bismarck"

5. Die Verfolger verlieren die Spur

6. „Bismarck" wieder aufgefunden; erfolgreicher Angriff der Torpedoflieger der „Ark Royal"

7. Das Ende der „Bismarck"

WESTLICHES
MITTELMEER-GESCHWADER

RENOWN

GIBRALTAR

The graphic (above) is how the Germans saw the operation. It's pretty accurate but doesn't make clear that carrier HMS *Ark Royal* came up from Gibraltar.

The dramatically short operational life and loss of *Bismarck* influenced subsequent use of slightly larger sister ship *Tirpitz*. Kriegsmarine finally had to recognize there was no longer a possibility of a capital ship roaming the Atlantic as a commerce raider.

Wilhelmshaven-built, and slightly larger than *Bismarck*, *Tirpitz* was launched in April 1939 and commissioned in late February 1941. After all that expense, he wouldn't sit idle.

65

Confrontation was obviously nearing when the battleship was observed in the Fitting Out Basin at Wilhelmshaven on 29 October 1940. Small scale imagery permitted ID but no analysis of the warship. Note superstructure shadow on the water.

Tirpitz ("A") was still in Bauhafen (fitting out basin) later in the year. "B" is Admiral Scheer.

It was expected Tirpitz would use the Kiel Canal to reach the Baltic for sea trials and sure enough he was seen at Kiel on 30 May 1941 (just three days after Bismarck was sunk).

The caption says Tirpitz (annotation "A") was "out of S. floating dock having gun turrets exercised for departure." He departed Kiel four days later. Annotation "B" is Heavy Cruiser Hipper. Admiral Scheer was also present farther up in the Kiel Inner Basin. The warships exercised in the Baltic, then went north to the Arctic.

By the time Tirpitz was ready for battle the number of heavy German surface units was down to three and, beyond sinking a Royal Navy carrier and battlecruiser, none of the seven big ships had achieved anything particularly impressive against other warships. A daring British Commando raid on 28 March 1942 destroyed the doors on Normandie Dock at Saint Nazaire, France. Since Tirpitz could no longer count on a refuge if damaged, a Bismarck-style foray into the Atlantic was no longer an option.

66

Tirpitz sheltered in far northern Norwegian fjords beyond the range of RAF heavy bombers as a constant threat to convoys. (Right) Aasfjord, 15 February 1942. Tight against the fjord wall and inside torpedo netting, the target could only be attacked from one axis by bombs. The location is interesting because the battleship appears to be facing the narrowing end of the fjord and could only be turned by backing some distance into wider waters.

Enlargement of the 15 February oblique imagery (below) gives one the best looks at *Tirpitz*. Small boats and rafts fore and aft were intended to disguise the hull shape and make the huge warship "blend" into the coast to confuse bomb-aimers. I doubt any PIs were fooled.

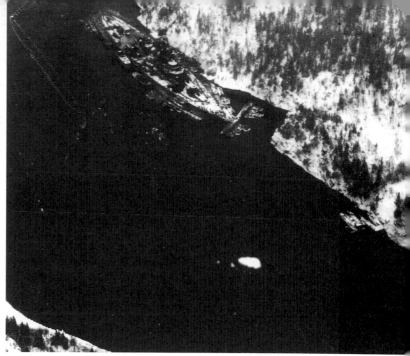

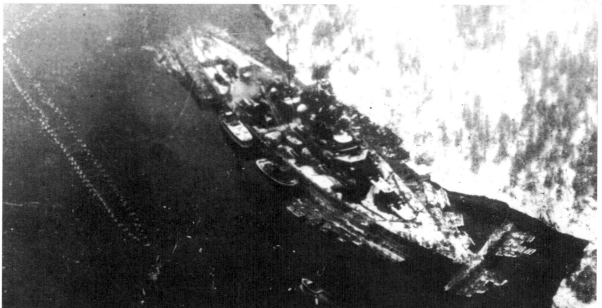

Tirpitz near 30 knots heading NE in Trondheim fjord, 19 February 1942. For some reason the forward turret is trained out to port.

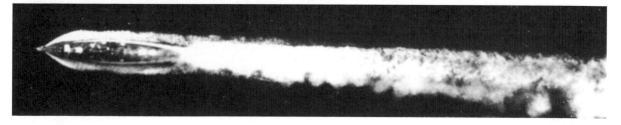

67

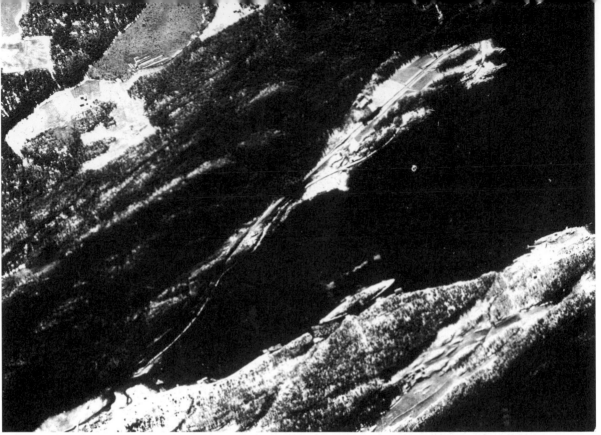

(Above) *Tripitz* was back in the Aasfjord anchorage on 30 April 1942.

Tirpitz fulfilled his purpose as a threat by sortieing against Convoy PQ-17 in June 1942, causing the convoy to scatter. Without escorts, twenty-four of the thirty-four freighters bound for Arkhangelsk, USSR fell prey to German submarines and land-based aircraft.

(Below) The battleship was imaged in Narvik's Bogen Fjord on 17 July 1942.

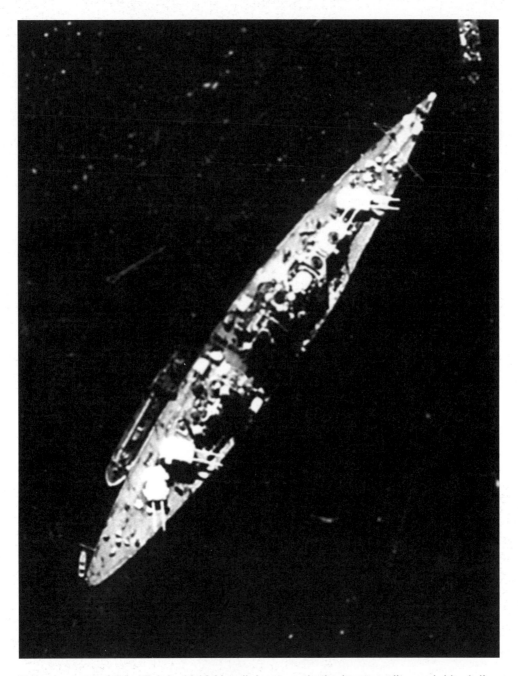

Enlargement of the 17 July 1942 Narvik imagery is the best quality aerial look I've ever seen of *Tirpitz* or any other German warship. Both aft and one forward turret are "exercising." The wide-spaced floats may be for an anti-torpedo net and the close-spaced floats for a heavier anti-submarine net.

Moving from fjord to fjord to avoid detection and remain a threat to Allied shipping, the battleship was located close to a steep rock incline on 16 December 1942. *Tirpitz* (arrow) had been painted dark gray or coated with coal-dust making him almost invisible. It is easier to see the accompanying freighter to the left. Masking smoke was mostly blowing the wrong way and only served to attract the 540Sq. PR pilot's attention.

A 543Sq. recce Mosquito found *Tirpitz* in Kaafjord (an arm of Alten Fjord), 23 September 1943. He was recently returned from a foray against Spitsbergen. This photo was taken the day after Royal Navy *X-craft* (miniature submarines) placed four two-ton Amatol charges under the battleship's hull, seriously damaging the BB and rendering Tirpitz unseaworthy until April 1944. The superstructure shadow helped identify this warship.

Tirpitz (top left) in the same position in Kaafjord, 5 October 1943. The Allies didn't know how badly the ship was hurt by the submarine mines. The larger of the side-by-side ships at lower right is probably *Scharnhorst*, just eight weeks away from his December sinking in the Battle of North Cape.

August saw *Tirpitz* at sea again and numerous attempts by many types of RAF and Royal Navy carrier planes to sink the battleship. A few sorties were even flown from temporary basing in the Soviet Union. They did enough damage to disable the ship again but failed to sink him. Here the battleship is being bombed in his Kaafjord anchorage.

In October there was so much hull damage that *Tirpitz* was sent to a bay four miles west of Tromso to act as a floating battery in anticipation of an Allied invasion. This put the battleship within range of RAF heavy bombers flying from Scotland and precipitated three attacks with 12,000 lb. "Tallboy" bombs between 15 September and 12 November 1944.

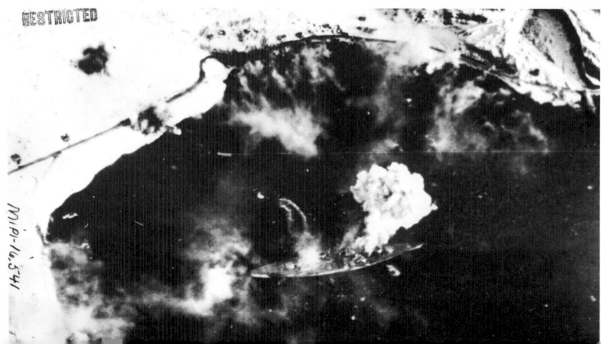

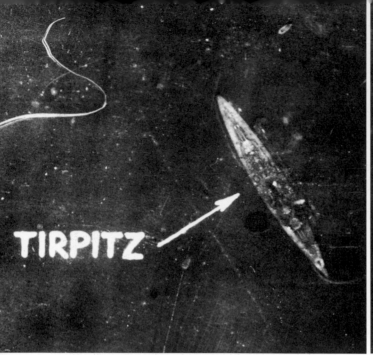
TIRPITZ

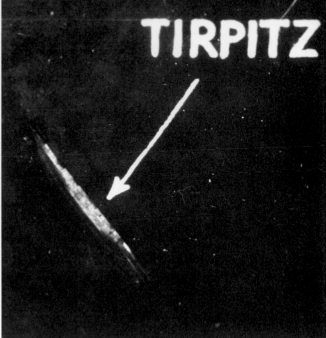
TIRPITZ

Enlargement of an RAF PR photo probably taken in early November. I can't tell if those dark spots beside the hull are craters from an earlier attack, oil leaking from the ship, or flaws on the negative).

On 12 November 1944 three 12,000 lb. bombs hit on or near the hull, capsizing the battleship with the loss of two-thirds of the crew

Right photo above, same location near Tromso, Norway sometime shortly after 12 November 1944.

(Below) German photo of crewmen on the hull, probably taken within a day of Tirpitz turning turtle.

72

AIRCRAFT CARRIER

Laid down at Kiel in 1936, the 861-foot long ship (23 feet longer than Tirpitz) was launched in December 1938. Loosely inspired by contemporary Japanese carriers, *Graf Zeppelin* suffered from a complete lack of carrier aviation experience and Reichsmarschall Göring's lack of interest in a Naval Air Arm competing with his Luftwaffe.

Work suspended in May 1940 and the ship was towed to Gdynia in July 1940.

In June 1941 it was moved to Stettin, out of bombing range of Soviet aircraft but was towed back to Gdynia again Nov 1941 where work could begin once more.

Graf Zeppelin was photographed at Kiel by 1PRU on 15 September 1941. He is heavily camouflaged in drydock but not fooling anyone. The characteristic shape and off-set superstructure can be seen at bottom left of the net-masked shape.

(Below) On 1 August 1942 he was back in Gdynia but not in the active part of the port where heavy work was done, signaling that construction was stalled again.

73

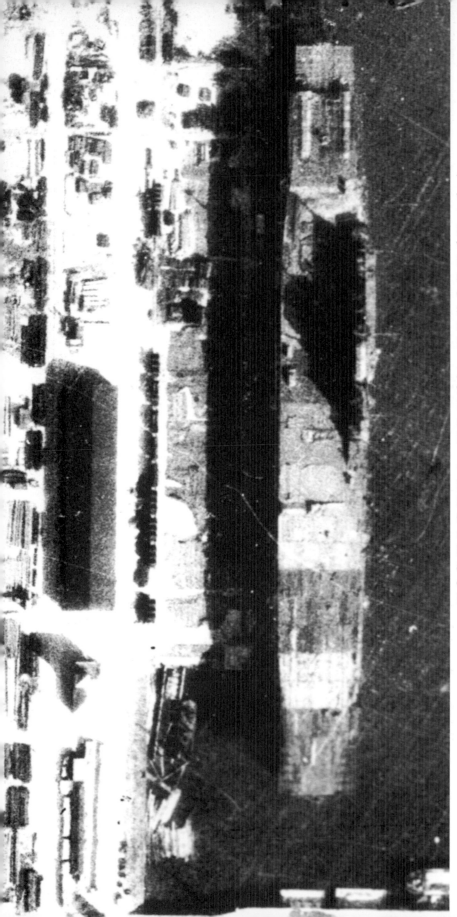

The best look at *Graf Zeppelin* was a 1PRU mission of 5 October 1942. He was still moored at the port "wood yard" indicating no work going on. Mats and netting have been added to bow (top) and stern in a crude attempt to disguise the ship but the superstructure shadow can't be misunderstood. The bow is facing photo top.

High level interest in *Graf Zeppelin* waxed and waned as the war progressed and carriers were increasingly important (sinking of *Bismarck*, Taranto, and Pearl Harbor).

Construction restarted in May 1942. Hull changes were required in the spring of 1942 to balance increasing top-heavy additions. Other major changes were required based upon lessons learned from Japanese, American and British carrier ops so the carrier was towed back to Kiel in December 1942.

Kiel, 1 January 1943. RAF photo interpreters annotated

"1. Forward and midships aircraft lift shafts.

2. Forward tower on deck.

3. Midships tower on deck.

4. After tower on deck.

5. Approximate position of the funnel."

In January 1943 Hitler was expressing disenchantment with his surface navy so work on the CV ended the following month.

I doubt this venture could have been successful. The intended Fieseler Fi 167 torpedo bi-planes were 100 knots slower than the intended Ju 87 dive-bombers (which had been pulled from the Battle of Britain as too slow to survive). The Messerschmitt Bf 109T fighter's narrow track landing gear would have turned a notoriously "hairy" landing on a normal field into a nightmare on a moving deck at sea. In addition, none of the air or naval personnel had any experience with Naval Air—no tactics, no procedures, no techniques.

With shore bases from Norway to Greece covering the Baltic, most of the Mediterranean and a good stretch of the Western Atlantic, where was ship-borne aviation required? The carrier wasn't going to sortie into the open Atlantic—Bismarck was faster and couldn't pull that off (the CV was planned for 35 knots but hull changes and added weight above the waterline make that doubtful, certainly not for any length of time). He wasn't going to transit Gibraltar into the Med.

By 1942 Graf Zeppelin had no mission.

In April 1943 Graf Zeppelin was briefly back in Gdynia, then on to Stettin and moored out of the way up a side-river.

75

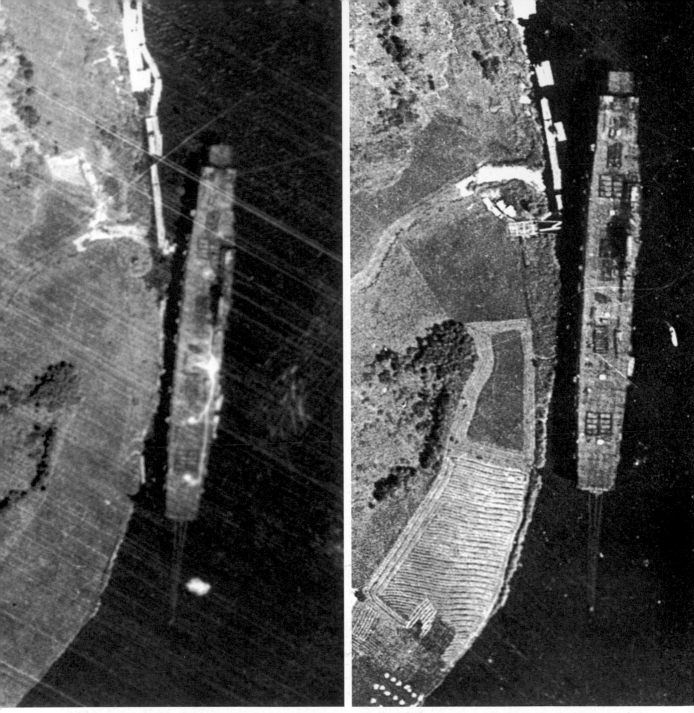

(Above left) Stettin, 26 July 1943. Something was happening on the deck. Apparently power or hose-lines had been run to four locations. The bow is facing north (toward the top of the photo) and mooring lines are at the stern because the river runs north to the Baltic.

(Above right) Stettin, 18 August 1943, the lines are no longer seen but their four terminals show as small white squares on the deck. The grid-work on deck is more apparent (it probably equates to the location of plane elevators). Curiously, all of these photos have false-work masking the shape of the bow, though what is accomplished by that on an easily identified derelict is obscure.

76

The unfinished carrier was left to rust alone at Stettin. The photo (below) is from 28 November 1943 and shows the true pointed bow configuration. I have nearly identical photos from several dates in 1944. *Graf Zeppelin* was covered frequently through early 1945 with no additional changes in position or status. He was scuttled in this location in April 1945 as Soviet troops neared the port. Refloated by the Soviets, the CV was a target ship sunk in deep water in 1947.

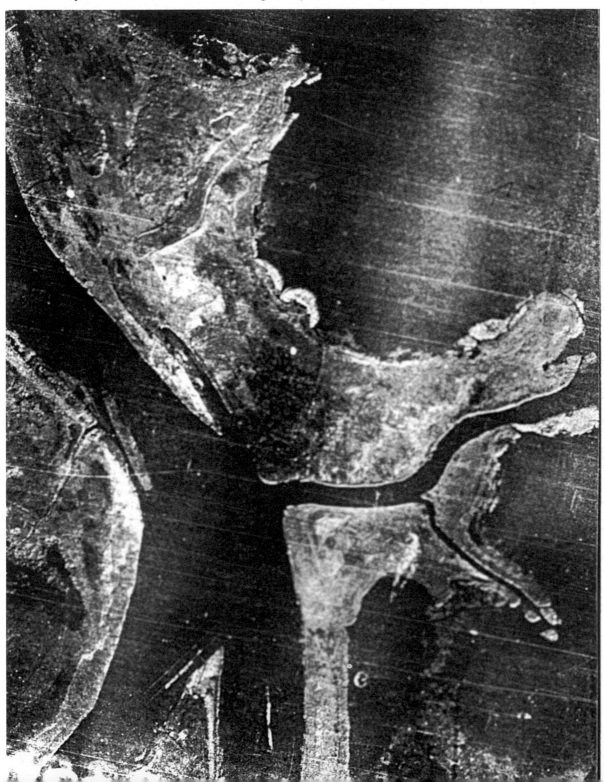

HEAVY CRUISERS

The German Navy began the war with three 8"-gun cruisers and two more building, all of the same class and design, though the final three would be heavier, 16 feet longer, two feet wider, have more armor, more AAA and greater range than the first two ships.

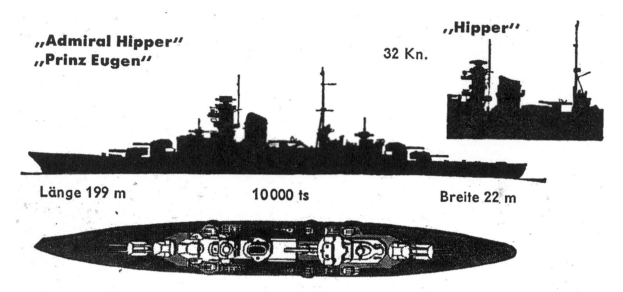

„Admiral Hipper"
„Prinz Eugen"

„Hipper"

32 Kn.

Länge 199 m   10 000 ts   Breite 22 m

Two heavy cruisers are shown on this Luftwaffe Recognition Guide printed in December 1940. *Lützow* was sold to the Soviets as part of the 1939 Nazi-Soviet Pact that carved up Poland. The incomplete CA was taken to Leningrad and renamed *Petropavlovsk* (the name *Lützow* then went to the Pocket Battleship *Deutschland*). Used as a floating battery against the German Invasion, the unready cruiser was reportedly sunk upright in shallow water at Kronstadt in June 1941, damaged by bombs again in April 1942 and not raised until September. He saw action as a floating battery later in 1942 and in 1944. The Luftwaffe photographed their former cruiser on 1 June 1942. The photo was annotated as Leningrad, and that doesn't look like anything I recognize at Kronstadt, nor does the ship appear sunk or damaged, so perhaps some of the conventional wisdom is wrong. Only the two lower turrets have guns but at least one appears workable.

78

Blücher (above) had the misfortune to be sunk by coastal artillery fire on its first outing—near Oslo on 9 April 1940 during the Invasion of Norway—so it was not mentioned in the Luftwaffe ship recognition guide above, but he did appear in pre-war materials. These cruisers shared the same clean, graceful silhouette of the battlecruisers.

In June 1942 Hitler decided he needed a fast, light aircraft carrier more than another heavy cruiser. In spite of the fact that *Seydlitz* was near completion it was chosen for conversion. Here he is at Bremen from a 5 June 1942 photo and PI Report. The annotations say the ship was "being dismantled," but all eight 8" guns are still in place.

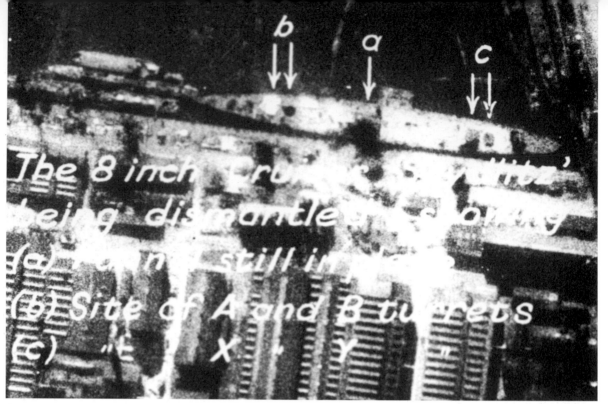

(Above) *Seydlitz* at Deschimag Yards, Bremen on 7 March 1943. The funnel hasn't been re-trunked to the side yet (to clear a carrier deck) but rapid progress is being made stripping off the superstructure. These annotations are a little premature implying that the turrets have been removed—the guns have been pulled but only the "B" turret is gone.

When the carrier conversion idea stalled, then fell through, *Seydlitz* was sent to Königsberg, East Prussia. Photographed there on 27 August 1944 (below), shadows show "A, X and Y" turrets in place but without guns. It also seems the quality of the Bremen imagery was too poor to make a more detailed photo interpretation—shadows show much of the superstructure still in place. He was scuttled here on 10 April 1945.

Class leader *Admiral Hipper* was very active and very successful early in the war, operating against Atlantic convoys with *Scharnhorst* and *Gneisenau* off Norway and in three solo Atlantic commerce raiding sorties from Brest, France between December 1940 and March 1941. Well within range of RAF photoreconnaissance, *Hipper* was carefully watched.

Above, Brest, 5 January 1941. The cruiser seemed to require a lot of drydocking following each sortie.

A better look took place a few days later, on 26 January 1941. This photo shows how low the PR Spitfire flew over the port, in spite of intense AAA fire.

81

Enlargement of the 26 January 1941 photo shows people on the ship and dock looking at the low fly-by. Note camouflage paint on hull and turrets, and rapid-fire guns trained out in the approach direction of the PR Spitfire (from the right). An Arado Ar 196 is on the catapult midships.

Hipper was damaged off Norway in late December 1942 and sat out much of the war at Gdynia. Some post-war sources say the cruiser wasn't active again until January 1945, but below he is off Helle on 3 August 1944.

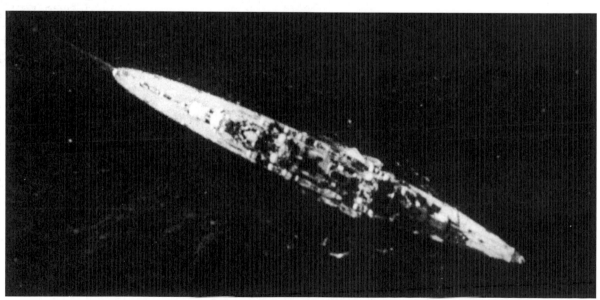

82

(Top) Submarines and *Hipper* at *Pillau* (Baltysk), East Prussia on 12 August 1944.

(Above) Enlargement. Unlike *Prinz Eugen*, as far as I've seen, *Hipper* never wore a Nazi herald on the bow.

(Right) Darkened for camouflage, *Hipper* was at Kiel on 22 March 1945, waiting for a drydock to be available.

Hipper in drydock at Kiel on 7 April 1945. Smoke heavy enough and low enough to pass under the large Hammer Head Crane shows it to be part of the passive defenses. Note the large U-boats afloat in the drydock just below *Hipper* and the bulbous hull-shapes of two subs out of the water in the next drydock up. Some of the cruiser's darkening camouflage is still apparent, but no attempt has been made to disrupt the shape to hinder identification from the air.

(Below) The drydock was still flooded on 22 April 1945 and there is no dock-side evidence of work in progress. Note superstructure shadow. The drydocked submarines haven't moved.

This photo must have been taken shortly after *Hipper* was scuttled in drydock at Kiel on 2 May 1945. Apparently some damage was also done to his 8" guns. The camouflage netting is a ridiculous attempt to hide the ship.

An OSS photo of 15 June 1945 (below) shows the netting removed and at least three men on *Hipper* examining the damage (look below the rear port side AAA guns). Note bomb damage to the dock wall opposite the turrets. At first glance it appears his back is broken. It isn't. The lines of the hull and deck are straight. That is the shadow of a wooden platform built to cover some port-side hull/deck damage.

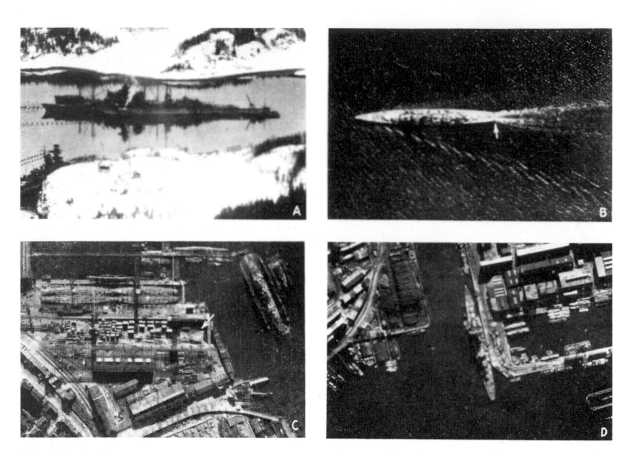

(A). The PRINZ EUGEN, with the HUASCARAN depot ship alongside, undergoing temporary repairs to her stern in LO FJORD after escaping from BREST and being torpedoed by H.M.S. TRIDENT on 21.2.42. (B). Under way off Norway on 17.5.42 while returning to KIEL: note stern temporarily squared off. (C). New stern being built at Germania Yard, KIEL. (D). PRINZ EUGEN in KIEL after having new stern fitted.

Though *Prinz Eugen* was known in the German Navy as a "Lucky Ship," he suffered hits by gunfire, torpedoes, bombs and at least one major collision at sea. He was never sunk. (Above) Are four photos put together for a British Intelligence publication documenting *Eugen*'s torpedoing and loss of his stern, then replacement at Kiel.

The enlargement below is from the original 1PRU imagery of 17 May 1942. *Eugen* is heading for shipyards at Kiel, making good speed in spite of his truncated stern.

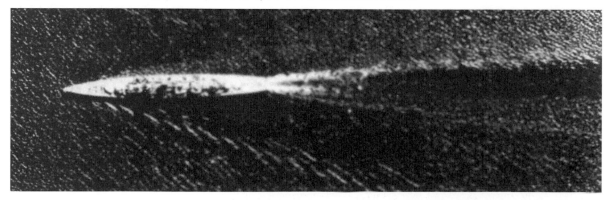

Fully operational, *Eugen* was at Gdynia on 10 October 1943, moored ahead of Light Cruiser *Emden*. The Nazi herald prominent on the bow deck became a PI recognition key for *Prinz Eugen* for most of the war.

Imaged on a regular basis in the Baltic and Gdynia, in 1944 the cruiser was active shelling advancing Soviet forces and escorting refugee ships west. On 15 October 1944 he collided with Light Cruiser *Leipzig*, suffering bow damage and putting the CL out of the war.

Bow repaired, *Prinz Eugen* was at sea off Gdynia on 24 March 1945, four days before his last refugee trip. The cruiser went to Swinemünde then Copenhagen. Stranded without fuel, *Eugen* was surrendered there to the Royal Navy on 8 May 1945.

Prinz Eugen as a prize after the war (probably at Wilhelmshaven). He was turned over to the US Navy and finally sank on 22 December 1946 during in a towing accident after surviving two Atomic Bomb tests in the Pacific.

LIGHT CRUISERS

At the start of World War II, Reichsmarine had six 6"-gun cruisers. Two of the "K-Cruisers" were gone by the time the Luftwaffe made their ship recognition aid in December 1940.

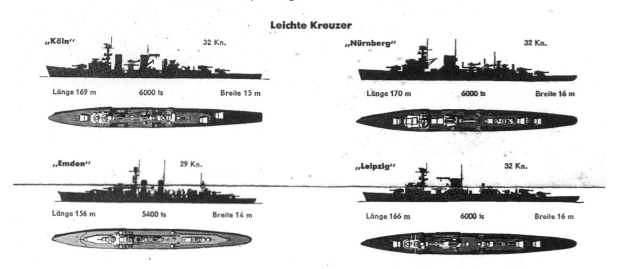

Leichte Kreuzer

„Köln" 32 Kn. Länge 169 m 6000 ts Breite 15 m

„Nürnberg" 32 Kn. Länge 170 m 6000 ts Breite 16 m

„Emden" 29 Kn. Länge 156 m 5400 ts Breite 14 m

„Leipzig" 32 Kn. Länge 166 m 6000 ts Breite 16 m

I'm repeating the 2 September 1944 photo of Gdynia (below) because it shows all but one of the remaining German CL. At upper left above the mole is *Köln*, easily recognized by the off-set rear turrets; past the hulk of *Gneisenau* on the far right is *Emden*. Below the mole, right behind the old Battleship *Schleswig-Holstein* is CL *Leipzig*.

Commissioned in 1925, *Emden* was obsolete before war began. Treaty limitations on weight forced him to have eight 6" guns inefficiently mounted in eight separate turrets—two well separated forward and aft and two at the corners on each side of the superstructure (they show as light round shapes). Gdynia, 3 August 1944. *Emden* took part in the Invasion of Norway then remained in the Baltic as a training ship based at Gdynia.

Damaged in a bombing attack on Kiel in early April 1945, he was towed north up the Estuary, to an out of the way bay opposite the northern entrance to the Kiel Canal and beached, then scuttled on 3 May.

Leichter Kreuzer „Karlsruhe", 6000 ts, 169 m lang

Neue Kennung (Unterscheidung von den anderen K-Kreuzern): Zwei Schornsteine mit Schrägkappe, der achtere kürzer.
Am achteren Schornstein ein zweiter Mast: Dreibein-Stengenmast mit anscheinend einziehbarer Funkstenge.

There were three "K-Cruisers" when the war began: *Karlsruhe*, *Königsberg* and *Köln*. Though commissioned ten years earlier they had many modern features. Arc-welding was used to cut down weight and their modern triple-gun turrets mounted the latest 6" guns (actually 5.9"), something German industry made exceptionally well. The "K-Cruisers" toured the world, patrolled off Iberia during the Spanish Civil War and participated in the Invasion of Norway.

A British submarine torpedoed *Karlsruhe* off Kristiansand on 9 April 1940. The crew was taken off and the crippled cruiser sunk by his escorts.

Also on 9 April (the day that all but sank the German surface Navy), *Königsberg* was damaged by coastal batteries defending Bergen. The next day Royal Navy Blackburn "Skua" dive bombers capsized the light cruiser.

An RAF PR Mosquito from Scotland took this photo of Bergen Harbor on 25 March 1943. The enlargement shows *Königsberg* upside down with three ships and fourteen floats being used to right the cruiser. Note the same salvage boats hovering around the CL in both photos. A shadow shows a substantial rectangular structure built on the center of the hull, seemingly attached to pipes running along the side of the ship.

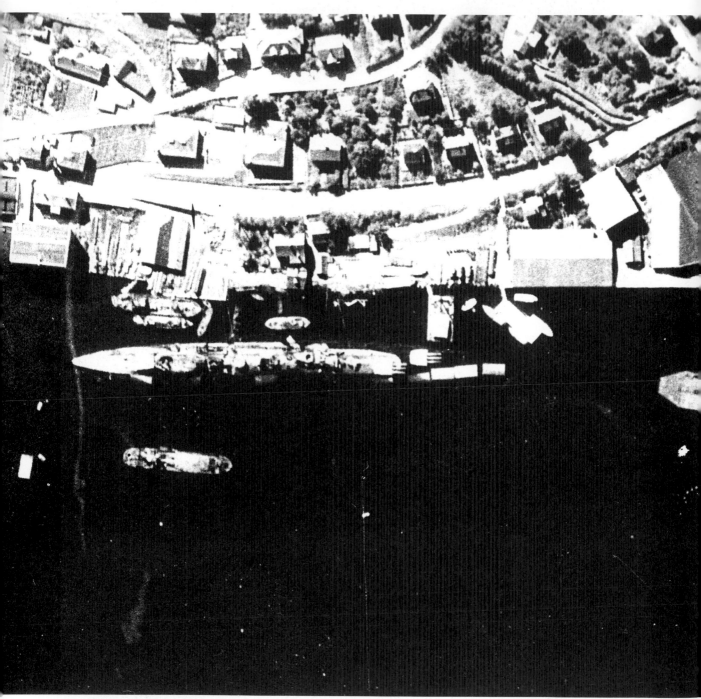

Königsberg was upright (but listing to port) when photographed on 18 July 1943. It had been successfully rolled towards the shore and shallower water. The stern, with its characteristic off-set turrets, is still under water. At least eight floatation devices are on the port side. The CL was used as a U-boat dock until he capsized again in September 1944.

90

Light Cruiser *Köln* led a charmed life, almost making it through the war. After the usual training, Spanish Civil War patrolling, and duty during the Invasion of Norway, he saw some service attacking and mining North Atlantic convoy routes. Sub torpedo damage in March 1943 caused *Köln* to be out of service for a year, moored at Gdynia as we have already seen. Bomb damage in December 1944 forced withdrawal to Wilhelmshaven for major repairs, where he was sunk in shallow water on 3 March 1945.

A 1PRU Spitfire found *Köln* in Foetten Fjord on 17 July 1943.

(Below) An enlargement shows an extensive torpedo net and serious attempts at disguising the shape of the CL, making him blend into the fjord wall—the unique off-set aft turrets show well.

People on the ground always think they can fool photo interpreters—they can't.

(Above) Light Cruiser *Leipzig* off Helle, 24 March 1945, apparently anchored. An upgraded design but little improved capability over the "*K-Cruisers*," (actually less range), *Leipzig* had the usual Spanish Civil War patrolling and Norway Invasion pedigree. He participated in the Invasion of the Soviet Union and remained in the Baltic, functioning as a training ship. Seriously damaged in a collision with *Prinz Eugen* in mid-October 1944, *Leipzig* stayed in or near Gdynia, shelling Soviet Armies from those waters in March 1945. He was moved to a bay north of Flensburg and there surrendered to British Forces. *Leipzig* was loaded with unwanted chemical munitions and sunk in deep water in December 1946.

The final Light Cruiser was *Nürnberg*, photographed at Swinemünde on 26 July 1943. Commissioned in 1935, this was the latest and best German CL—basically an up-grade of *Leipzig*'s design but with the same main armament, and less range than a "K-Cruiser." Arrows show recognition points for the differences. *Nürnberg* had an additional AAA gun behind the aft 88mm double-gun turrets.

Nürnberg was not a lucky ship. In operation just in time for four two-month Spanish patrols, he was torpedoed by a British sub in mid-December 1939 and missed the Invasion of Norway. From July 1940 to January 1945 *Nürnberg* was either off Norway or in the Baltic, with no distinguished battles or accomplishments. At the end of WW II, the cruiser was surrendered at Copenhagen with *Prinz Eugen*, awarded to the Soviets as a prize and renamed *Admiral Makarov*.

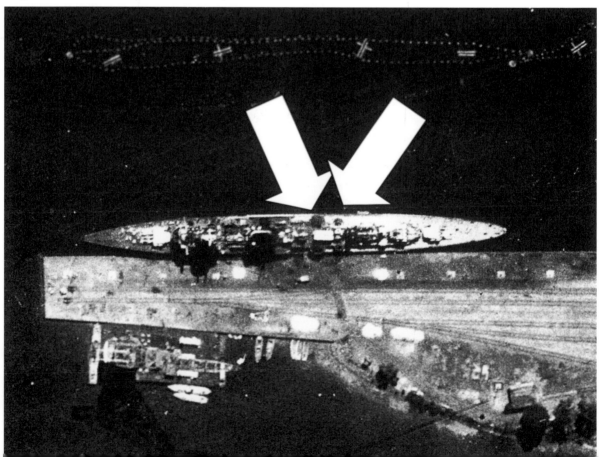

OTHER SURFACE SHIPS

Germany had all the usual compliment of lesser and ancillary ships, many of them showing on imagery earlier in this book. Back to our old friend the 1 December 1940 Luftwaffe warship recognition guide.

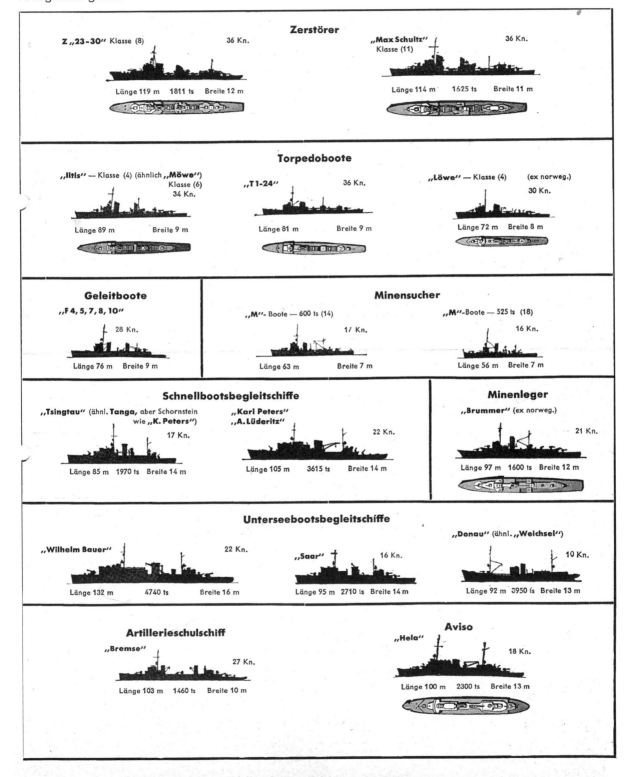

Zerstörer

Z „23-30" Klasse (8)　　36 Kn.
Länge 119 m　1811 ts　Breite 12 m

„Max Schultz" Klasse (11)　36 Kn.
Länge 114 m　1625 ts　Breite 11 m

Torpedoboote

„Iltis" — Klasse (4) (ähnlich „Möwe") Klasse (6)　34 Kn.
Länge 89 m　Breite 9 m

„T 1-24"　36 Kn.
Länge 81 m　Breite 9 m

„Löwe" — Klasse (4)　(ex norweg.)　30 Kn.
Länge 72 m　Breite 8 m

Geleitboote

„F 4, 5, 7, 8, 10"　28 Kn.
Länge 76 m　Breite 9 m

Minensucher

„M"- Boote — 600 ts (14)　17 Kn.
Länge 63 m　Breite 7 m

„M"-Boote — 525 ts (18)　16 Kn.
Länge 56 m　Breite 7 m

Schnellbootsbegleitschiffe

„Tsingtau" (ähnl. Tanga, aber Schornstein wie „K. Peters")　17 Kn.
Länge 85 m　1970 ts　Breite 14 m

„Karl Peters" „A. Lüderitz"　22 Kn.
Länge 105 m　3615 ts　Breite 14 m

Minenleger

„Brummer" (ex norweg.)　21 Kn.
Länge 97 m　1600 ts　Breite 12 m

Unterseebootsbegleitschiffe

„Wilhelm Bauer"　22 Kn.
Länge 132 m　4740 ts　Breite 16 m

„Saar"　16 Kn.
Länge 95 m　2710 ts　Breite 14 m

„Donau" (ähnl. „Weichsel")　10 Kn.
Länge 92 m　3950 ts　Breite 13 m

Artillerieschulschiff

„Bremse"　27 Kn.
Länge 103 m　1460 ts　Breite 10 m

Aviso

„Hela"　18 Kn.
Länge 100 m　2300 ts　Breite 13 m

Zerstörer „23-30", 1800 t, 36 Kn, 119 m lang, 12 m breit. Bewaffnung: Vorerst 4/15
(später auf der Back Doppel-Geschütz).
Kennung: Ähnlich „Karl Galster" („Diether v. Roeder"- Klasse), jedoch vorne nur ein Geschütz.

I confess to having specific interest in the larger ships, so I didn't keep many photos of the lesser vessels I was coming across thirty years ago (remember, these are not all the photos there were—just a few of the copies I kept because they caught my eye).

By all accounts German destroyers were 36 knot but lightly gunned, good ships and well handled, but there weren't many of them and without "heavy-ships" leading an attack there was little they could do offensively and no particular mission on the defense. Allied Intelligence kept track of them anyway since their movements could be indicators.

(Below) 34 knot *Möwe*-class Motor Torpedo Boats (largest of their type), probably an Attaché photo from before the war. The foreground ship, *Falke*, took part in the Invasion of Norway, laid mines off Dover and was sunk by bombs at Le Havre on 14 June 1944.

Torpedoboot „T 1" (-8), 600 ts, 81 m lang

Kennung: Ein Schornstein. Durchgehendes Deck. Schornstein und Kommandobrücke im vorderen Drittel. Auf der Back kein Geschütz. Schornstein ist breiter und weiter vorlich als bei neuen Minensuchbooten.

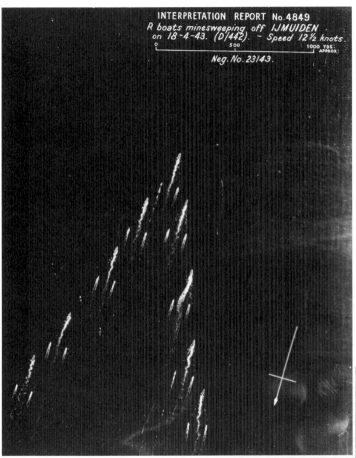

INTERPRETATION REPORT No. 4849
R boats minesweeping off IJMUIDEN
on 18-4-43. (D/442). – Speed 12½ knots.
0   500   1000 YDS. APPROX.
Neg. No. 23143.

German boats mined and de-mined the English Channel on a regular basis to make it safe for friendlies and more dangerous for foes. The nine *R-boats* (left) are each towing two paravanes in a classic "sweep pattern." Photo Interpreters calculated the speed by the length of wakes.

Torpedo boats, *E-boats* (similar to American PTs and British MTBs) and mine-layers were active all along the Atlantic coast from Germany to the Bay of Biscay, acting as "foragers" and "scouts" as they harassed any Allied vessels that came within range and helped defend ports from Commando attacks.

(Below) British Beaufighters attacking German mine-layers in the Gironde Estuary with rockets (three in the air on the left and four on the right of the photo.

(Above) Seaplane Tender *Friesland* with a Blohm & Voss Ha 139 floatplane aboard.

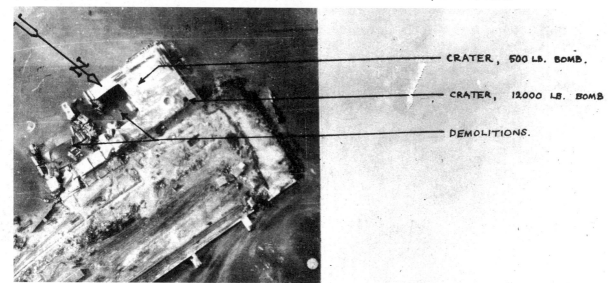

CRATER, 500 LB. BOMB.

CRATER, 12000 LB. BOMB

DEMOLITIONS.

"*E-boats*" weren't going into deep water to attack Atlantic convoys but they did attack ships plying the English Channel or trying to enter ports on the south coast of England.[3] They were a thorn in the side of Allied plans for the Normandy Invasion and were treated accordingly. This is coverage of *E-boat* pens at Le Havre on 6 October 1944.

(Right) Pre-*Dreadnought* BB SMS *Zähringen*, converted into a radio controlled target ship before the war. Aerial bombing sank him at Gdynia in December 1944. He was raised and scuttled as a blockship in the channel on 26 March 1945. March 1948 photo.

Sketch No. 1

Sketch No. 2

From: M/A, Berlin, Germany Report No. 18,248 May 9, 1941.

Auf dem weiten Meere werden diese Bojen. die Generalluftzeugmeister Generaloberst Udet einrichtete, den tapferen Fliegern willkommen sein. die „lahmgeschossen" wurden

Though not strictly naval vessels, I found the two photos above interesting. Both probably originated in German magazines and were sent to Washington by the U.S. Army Attaché in Berlin; the first from 9 May 1941, the second from 19 June 1941 (when the U.S. was still "neutral").

These modified buoys were intended to shelter pilots shot downed over the North Sea and English Channel. Pilot activated beacons would vector rescue seaplanes to the buoys so the pilots could be returned to German territory and cockpits.

A final surface vessel that caught my eye was on an enlargement of Stralsund from 26 July 1943. The full-rigged ship is probably the original *Gorch Fock*.

SUBMARINES

Undersea boats were a different world, fighting a different way, carrying the war to the very shores of the enemy, threatening to strangle aid to Britain and the Soviet Union by interdicting American and Commonwealth intervention. The Allies knew how serious the U-boat threat was and reacted accordingly. The main arena for this momentous game was the North Atlantic. The players were U-boats, spies in Allied ports, radio intercepts and long-range reconnaissance planes from France and Norway versus merchant ships, their escorts, Signals Intelligence and patrol aircraft from the U.S., Canada, Greenland, Iceland and the UK. Had Hitler put his chips here instead of wasting huge amounts of time, manpower, resources and wealth on surface ships (and a host of other programs with little chance to be decisive) the course of the war might have been quite different.

Early in the war many U-boat captains operated like the "commerce raiders," stopping merchant ships while surfaced, putting the crews in lifeboats then sinking the ships with gunfire.

Grouping ships in large convoys was a way to make best use of the available escorts and minimize losses, but it also provided submarines that found them a "target rich" environment. Much like Wildebeests crossing a crocodile infested river, it was hoped most freighters would complete the journey safely.

With losses rapidly mounting, many cargo ships were hastily armed with WW I vintage ordnance—in this case probably a 3" gun. Near the British West Indies, 14 November 1942.

A few guns on freighters deterred surface attack, forcing subs under where they were slower. That armament wasn't much real protection against U-boats. This is the bow half of a torpedoed tanker abandoned and adrift near the British West Indies, 13 September 1942.

More convoys, more subs, and the Royal Navy was being stretched thinner with each new day of war. American "Lend Lease" sent one hundred WW I-vintage destroyers to help.[4] The venerable four-stackers served well but were barely a match for a U-boat.

USS *Blakeley* (DD 150) was the only four-stacker to survive a torpedo hit. She lost 60 feet of bow on 5 May 1942. After installation of a temporary bow in the British West Indies, she was photographed on 27 May 1942 on her way to the Philadelphia Navy Yard.

(Below) Anti-submarine warfare was in its infancy when this photo was taken on 18 August 1940. Rolling depth-charges off a fantail gave a narrow "kill pattern" requiring precision tracking of submerged subs that Allied ships simply couldn't do well at the time.

U-boats sometimes met at sea to trade supplies information, or join to attack a detected convoy. Long-range Luftwaffe patrol planes helped spot targets for them. But each message for a rendezvous or attack might be intercepted and lead a surface hunter-killer team to a U-boat.

By 1943, submarine detection and depth-charging was becoming an art and convoys had ships like the *Black-Swan*-class sloop HMS *Starling* roving around them as "free hunters." This ship participated in the sinking of fifteen subs during the war.

Highly vulnerable on the surface, especially entering or leaving port, U-boats had to be constantly alert for air attack. Oilskins and binoculars were the rule.

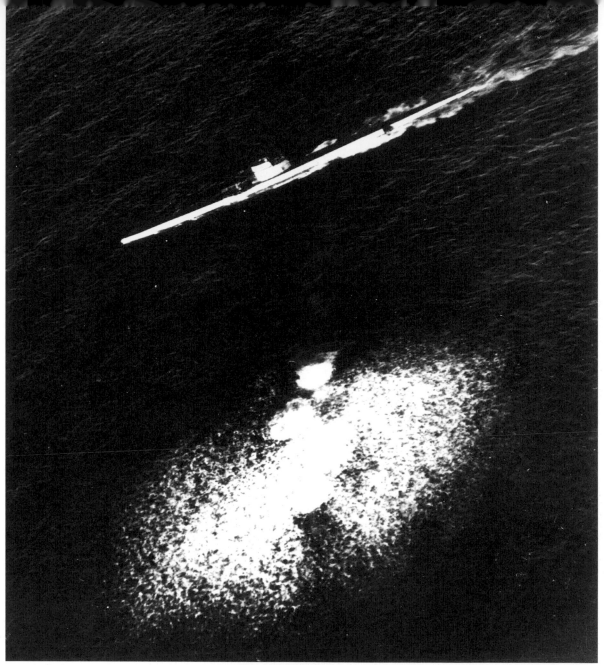

Surface engagements were fleeting so Allied photos of U-boats were few and far between in the files I screened. One of the earliest I found was of a 1 July 1940 Sunderland flying-boat attack on a sub some 200 miles south of Ireland. The sub, from a German port this early in the war, was hunting in sea lanes to Southampton and Liverpool. The bombs aren't close and it looks like men are still on the conning tower. I don't pretend to be good on ID-ing subs, but I'd call this a Type VII boat.

Dangerous as sharks submerged, submarines were at terrible risk if caught on the surface, particularly by aircraft. If radar or high-powered Leigh lights could spot a surfaced sub the aircraft had a great speed and maneuverability advantage, and easily out-gunned all but a few of the U-boats—and the areas covered by Allied air patrols were expanding. Even small damage to the hull could force a submarine to remain surfaced and vulnerable.

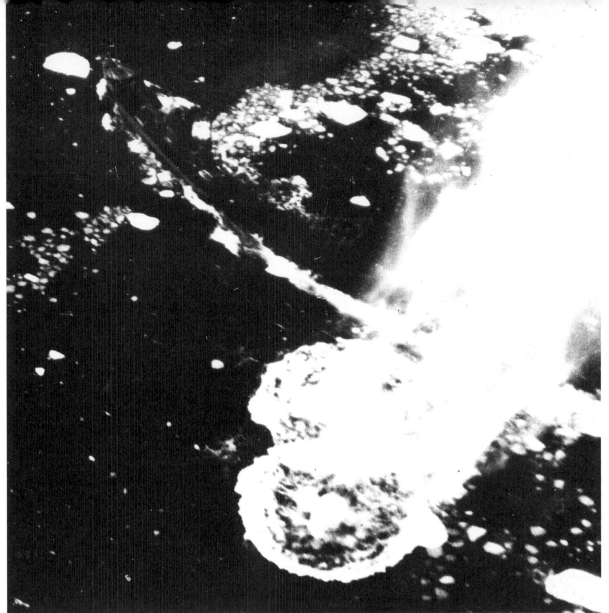

(Above) Another near miss, this time in ice off the southern tip of Norway on 16 February 1941. The rising bow line and small conning tower suggest a Type IX boat.

(Right) Appears to be another VIIc boat (probably *U-705*) submerging in the Bay of Biscay under depth charge attack by an Armstrong Whitley (identified by the unique vertical stabilizer), 3 September 1942. The sub reportedly went down with all hands.[5] Obsolescent Whitleys had only recently entered Coastal Command service.

(Right) This may be VIIC boat 617, disabled by aerial depth-charging the U-boat was run aground off Spanish Morocco on 12 September 1943 and later destroyed by Royal Navy surface craft.

U-boats ranged from the Caribbean to the British West Indies and great success against merchant traffic off the East Coast of the U.S. as well as Atlantic shipping lanes. Depth charges straddle this sub (probably a XIc) about 350 miles east of the southern tip of Greenland on 23 April 1943. Defenders were gradually gaining the upper hand in that year.

Inflatable life rafts are in the water as the crew abandons their Type VIIC boat west of the Azores. U-664 is sinking by the stern after strafing by aircraft from CVE USS *Card* on 9 August 1943.

Three men in life vests are on the conning tower with another rubber raft as the hull is going under.

The 9th Unterssbootsflottille, based at Brest, France, used a Sawfish as their emblem.

U-boats sometimes teamed up at sea but I believe the photo above is a double-exposure taken during an attack (hand cocked aerial cameras were often used in bombers). This negative had no information on date or location.

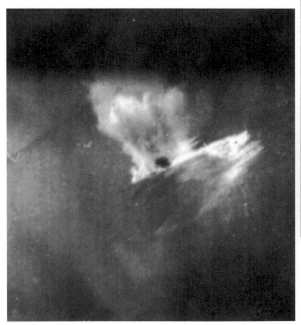

The photos above and left are of an attack on a submerging U-boat 500 miles SW of Iceland on 17 October 1943. The explosion looks like a hit. This may be a Type VII boat during the U-boat Arm "Autumn Offensive."

106

Avoiding Allied air interference when they had a chance, submarines made secret rendezvous with supply ships to extend their sortie or get a faster "turn around" for the next one. Here torpedoes are being transferred to a U-boat in Lofjord (near Trondheim).

(Below) The photo caption said "VIII BC bombing sub-pens at Lorient, 21 Oct 42." Bombs are actually falling on a bunkered storage facility. The sub-pens are under construction at lower right. You can see the individual slips where the roof isn't finished. Sub-pens normally had wet-slips and some that could become drydocks for major repairs.

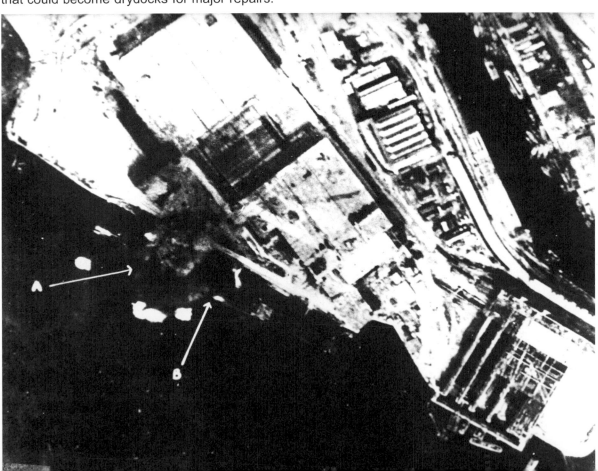

On 17 May 1943 the Lorient sub-pens were completed but apparently just as hard for the USAAF to hit. Bombs are all detonating just above the concrete pens sticking out into the estuary. Lorient was the largest U-boat complex in France.

(Below) Lorient, 10 August 1944, showing damage to the partially incomplete new roof. The U-boats had been pulled out three days earlier as Allied ground forces advanced.

Bomb damage to V-weapons bunkers and E/U-boat pens convinced German engineers that heavier roofs were required. Here we see the Lorient's second roof during installation with a clear space/crush zone to dampen penetration by heavy bombs. Roof thickness increased throughout the war, from 1.5 meters to 7.5 or more, but bomb penetration capability increased faster.

(Below) Securely inside a sub-pen, probably during the "Second Happy Times" (Die Glückliche Zeit of January to August 1942). Insignia on the sail at left says this is *U-270*, a Type VIIC boat sunk in August 1944.

109

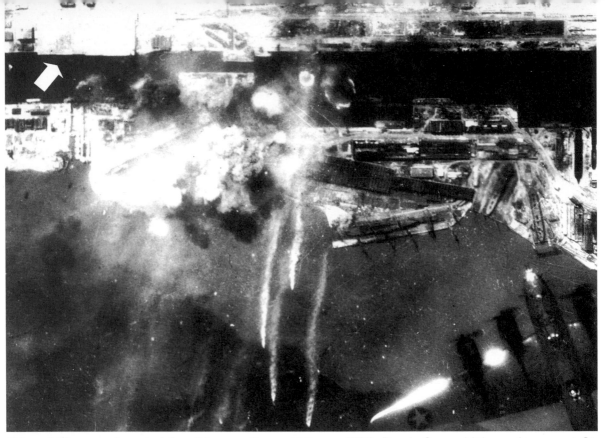

(Above) The envelope holding this negative said it was "79th Bomb Group hitting sub pens at St. Nazaire on 20 May 1942." Actually the bombs are hitting the *Normandie* Dock not the U-boat pens across the canal at upper left (arrow) and the B-17E was likely from 97th Bomb Group, some elements of which had arrived in the UK in early May. American bombers supposedly first operated against Occupied Europe on 17 August. Is this a bad date: an early USAAF "orientation" mission: Allied misinformation/propaganda: or history rewritten?

(Below) Splashes in the water and smoke in the town show the *Normandie* Dock is getting hammered but the sub-pens are escaping most of the damage.

Good coverage of the entire basin shows the U-boat pens as a white rectangle at lower left. I believe I see a faint shadow of HMS *Campbeldown* (ex-USS *Buchanan*) at the lower end of the angling *Normandie* Dock. On 28 March 1942, in a daring commando raid (Operation Chariot), the old destroyer, loaded with explosives, was rammed into the drydock's sea-gates. When she detonated it rendered the dock inoperative for the duration of the war—denying BB *Tirpitz* a haven to refit on the Atlantic coast.

A post-war OSS photo of St. Nazaire shows damage to the sub-pens roof and creation of a bunker over the locks across from the pens, leading straight out into the Atlantic, without which the U-boats could have been trapped inside the basin. Normandie Dock angles at the right. The town behind the bunker has suffered considerable damage.

111

Another post-war look at the St. Nazaire sub-pens shows the roof thickening incomplete. The completed lock bunker across the basin had a four-gun battery of AAA guns on the far end of the roof.

The graphic below shows what the Allies knew about U-boat pens in February 1943. Unfortunately, the author is noted but not his organization.

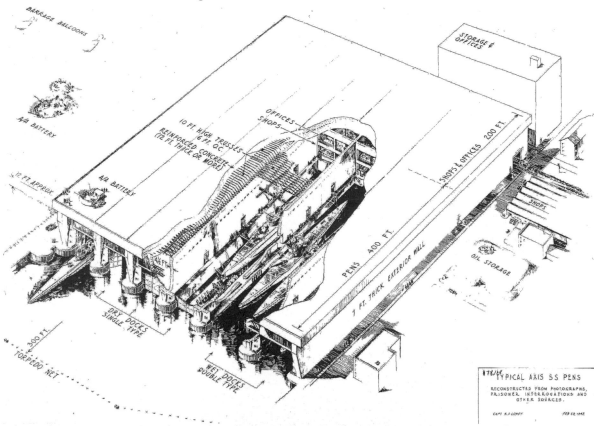

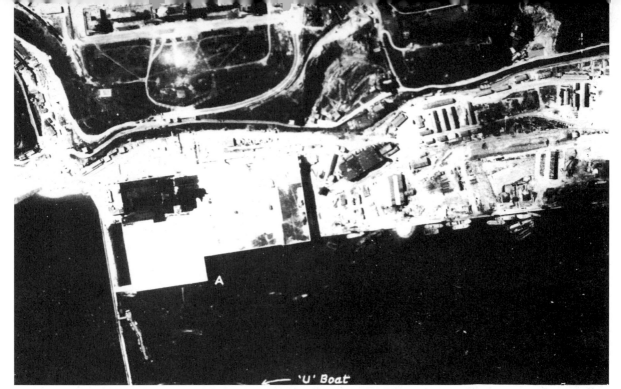

A   — 'U' Boat

Sub-pens at Brest, France (A) had slips of two different lengths. Absence of a wake suggests the annotated submarine was on its way in when the PR aircraft went over. Imagery quality and titling on the negative indicates the photo was probably sent to Washington by the USN Attaché in London and dates from before the U.S. entered the war—probably late 1941.

Below is a post-war photo showing damage to a bunker roof—in this case the E-boat pens at Le Havre. Scaling from the men on the roof, the concrete is between nine and ten feet thick. This is a lesson for military today. Bunkers may be effective avoiding loss of assets in a surprise attack but over a longer time they are as vulnerable as medieval castles became after use of gunpowder—as proven by war since WW II, better "penetrators" can be made faster and cheaper than one can pour concrete and bunkers actually concentrate and pin-down important targets for destruction in an air attack.

(Above) Cherbourg, 30 June 1944. Not all the U-boat and E-boat facilities were "hardened." This post-occupation OSS shot shows "Interior of damaged covered slip on south side of Avant-port in Port Militaire. Note torpedoes."

To my eye those torpedoes look more like high-pressure oxygen tanks. If 21" torpedo components, they scale out at 16.5 feet long.

(Left) Cherbourg on the same day. "Naval mines in freight cars in Gare Maritime."

Ijmuiden, Netherlands, 26 March 1944 showing the intensity of persistent bombing that impeded German naval operations—in this case "E/R-boat pens." The annotations indicate bomb hits from the most recent airstrike. (It was fun matching many of the photos in this book with current Google satellite imagery to verify locations. I found Ijmuiden one of the most changed areas, but the large German bunker at annotation "A" is still there and still showing roof damage).

115

Photograph N°2
GERMANIA YARD, KIEL
8.5.42. Photo 5226
Neg. N° 27775

740 Ton Minelaying U Boats fitting out. Note different appearance of the raised casings

(Above) A PI report of the same facility using 8 May 1942 imagery, highlighting large, special purpose U-boats (the image is turned because of writing—North is down).

As the Allied air offensive gained momentum, submarine building was pulled deeper into the Baltic to less vulnerable ports. At right is 12 April 1942 cover of Kiel. Sheds and drydocks for submarines were circled by an RAF photo interpreter.

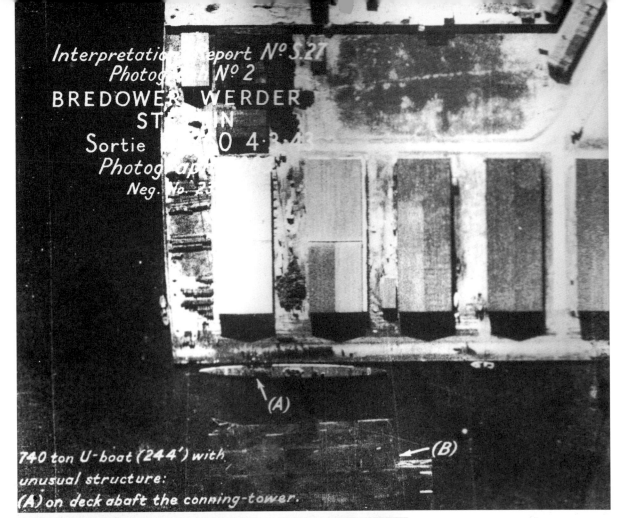

Interpretation Report Nº S.27
Photograph Nº 2
BREDOWER WERDER
STETTIN
Sortie ... 0 4 3 43
Photograph ...
Neg. No. 23

(A)

(B)

740 ton U-boat (244') with
unusual structure:
(A) on deck abaft the conning-tower.

(Above) Farther west, at Stettin on 3 April 1943, British PIs spotted another U-boat with unusual activity. It is interesting that Allied Intelligence named subs by length or displacement, not class. One has to wonder what's under that floating camouflage.

Even deeper into the Baltic, at Danzig, submarine construction, fitting out and training went on through the war. This 27 August 1944 cover shows twenty U-boats, four in floating drydocks. The larger ones are "Atlantic" boats. Smaller subs are "Baltic" boats used mainly for training.

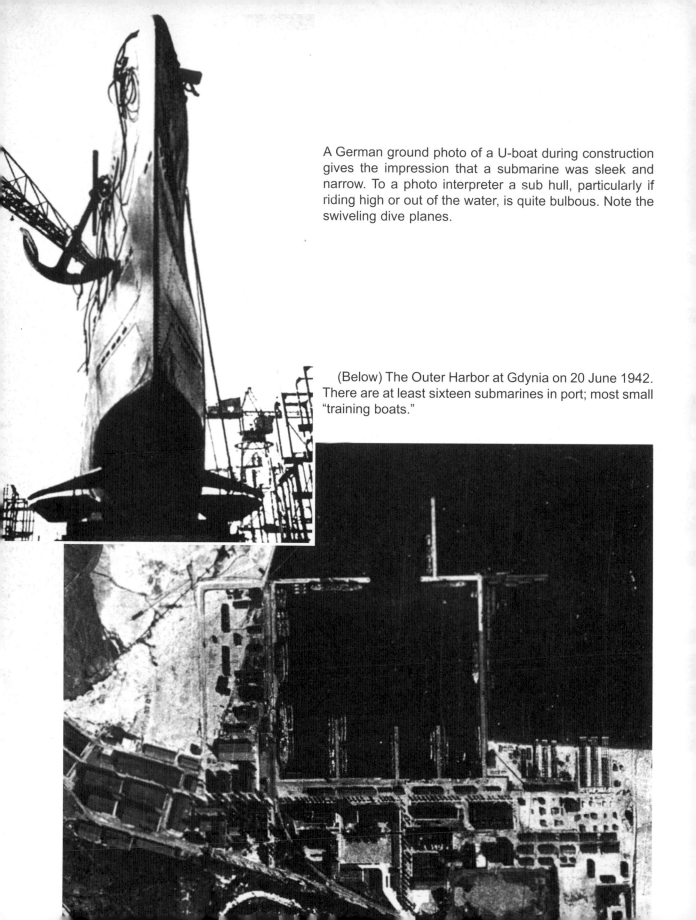

A German ground photo of a U-boat during construction gives the impression that a submarine was sleek and narrow. To a photo interpreter a sub hull, particularly if riding high or out of the water, is quite bulbous. Note the swiveling dive planes.

(Below) The Outer Harbor at Gdynia on 20 June 1942. There are at least sixteen submarines in port; most small "training boats."

Gdynia, 27 October 1944.

Thirteen U-boats are in the open including two at top center ready to sortie. The camera looks through the camouflage netting to reveal another nine submarines. Note there are more of the larger submarines this time.

U-boat construction got steadily better and faster throughout the war, so did submarine design. One of the most important innovations was the Snorkel (Schnorchel in German). Copied from a captured Dutch sub, it permitted fresh air to be drawn into the diesel motors and exhaust to go to the surface, allowing the sub to run submerged longer—and safer from attack. Tested in the Baltic in 1943, it was retrofit into VII and IX boats and most U-boats in the Atlantic were so equipped by 1944.

This photo shows USN personnel aboard a Type IX boat after the war. This Snorkel could be lowered into that recess in the deck just in front of it. Later subs were built with more effective telescoping Snorkels.

Below may be a photo of an "Elektroboot," the first true undersea warship. Snorkel-equipped, these subs were capable of remaining submerged for long periods running at 12 knots, making them safer from prowling radar-equipped aircraft.[6]

120

Many operational submarines not sunk by bombing were destroyed rather than surrendered. A post-war photo shows Type XXI U-boats, in various stages of completion, abandoned on their ways. Note the inner and outer hulls and six torpedo tube openings on the boat at rear center.

Below is Hamburg on 27 May 1945.

121

Biber (beaver) was a one-man mini-sub that was extensively deployed late in the war but saw few accomplishments. Concave shapes on each side were to hold torpedoes.

Below, *Neger* (Negro) was named for its inventor, Richard Mohr (whose name means negro in polite German). The one-man torpedo was ridden to the attack by a "frogman" with the upper one providing propulsion and the lower the detonation. This example was found at Anzio, Italy.

I'm not aware of *Neger* achieving anything notable. In a real sense a weapon like this demonstrates the frustration and hopelessness of a German war machine flailing about for something decisive—something that would reverse the increasingly crushing reality of a war that had turned solidly against them.

I want to mention one final German Naval initiative—Atlantic weather stations. Most weather in Europe comes from the west and German naval and air operations were at a disadvantage by not having current information to predict what was coming. They worked to intercept (and decode when necessary) radioed Allied weather reports, but badly wanted observations stations of their own in the western Atlantic. Starting in the 1920s, Canada, Denmark and Norway had maintained weather stations on Newfoundland, Greenland and Iceland (in the mid-1930s they also became valuable aerial navigation aids for planes crossing the North Atlantic).

Early in the war the U.S. Coast Guard and Canadian Navy began frequent air and sea patrols to deny the Nazis North Atlantic weather stations and German submarines attempted to plant both manned and unmanned stations.[7] Those stations were eliminated by the Allies as fast as they were found.

The 28 October 1942 photo (below) is representative of a site and the landscape. It is from Ella Island on Davy Sound—the east coast of Greenland (7250N 02515W). This radio/weather station was operated by Danes but a USCG cutter caught Germans posing as Norwegians in a trawler nearby in September 1942. Absorbed into the Allied reporting net, this station became "Bluie East 4." German lack of good weather prediction information from Greenland was a critical disadvantage during the days leading up to the Normandy Invasion.

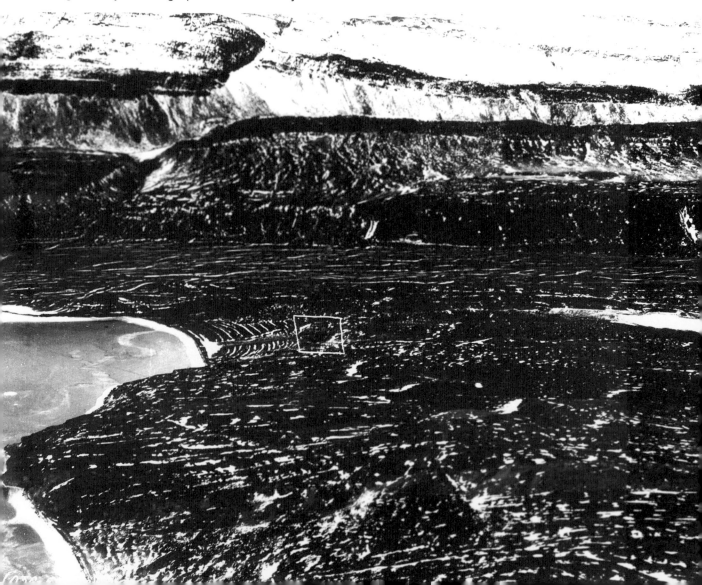

FOOTNOTES

[1]Roll Aerial film of *Gneisenau* at Gdynia was one of the first I saw as I reviewed "old missions" for possible destruction. The ship didn't look right with its strange bow and missing turrets. Researching for answers started me on digging into WW 2 from the air, a love affair that continues today almost three decades later.

[2]Only the five Royal Navy BB of *King George V*-class could run with *Bismarck.*

[3]It was E-boats that interrupted the US D-Day rehearsal at Slapton Sands on 28 April 1944, killing 749 GIs.

[4]This particular flush-deck (four-pipe) DD is *Clemson*-class USS *Zane.* She served in the Pacific during WW II. USS *Reuben James* was a *Clemson*-class DD.

[5]Some sources now say it was *U-660* and there were no hits.

[6]Please, U-boat mavens, the book is published. Tell each other if I'm wrong on some boat type IDs.

[7]I must have come across (but didn't screen) over 200 cans of 1942-43 aerial film from those Davis Strait air patrols. The few I did look at were nothing more than ice, snow, rocks and more ice—more boring PI than having to scan endless rolls of jungle in Southeast Asia. One has to admire the patience of the people who scanned that film.

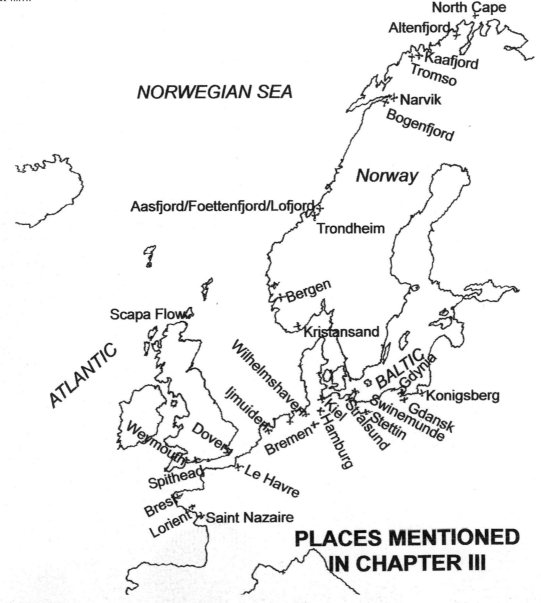

PLACES MENTIONED IN CHAPTER III

CHAPTER IV
REGIA MARINA

Italy had colonial interests but didn't aspire to be a global sea power. The French Navy in the Med was their natural naval adversary. War saw Italian naval units active in the Far East, off East Africa and in the Atlantic, but their goal was to be masters of the Mediterranean Sea, putting them on a collision course with Britain's Royal Navy. British bases at either end of the Med (Alexandria/Port Said and Gibraltar) controlled access but Italy counted on the number of British warships actually in the Med being limited by commitments across the globe. The rise of airpower, and their excellent strategic position, gave Italian naval forces a theoretical advantage for concentration of force. Focus on the long narrow Sea almost bisected by the Apennine Peninsula permitted the Italian navy to build ships with substantial armor and gun power but without the weight and space requirements for long range.[1] Lighter loads for accommodations, fuel and provisions let them be faster. Italy had some of the fastest warships afloat in every class—but they were unprepared for the war. Air-sea operations were poorly coordinated and Italian naval leadership had little experience in modern sea warfare, issuing directives that led to disaster. In addition, the British were regularly reading encrypted Italian naval message traffic.

Here are Battleships *Conte di Cavour*, *Gulio Cesare* and two *Castore*-class torpedo boats photographed in 1938, crewmen assembled aft indicates this was during a Naval Review.

When the Fascists came to power, Italy had four battleships of WWI vintage. They were stripped to their hulls in the mid-30s. Original mid-ships triple turrets were removed and all four BB were given new main and secondary batteries, more armor and larger power plants, bringing them up to the standards of modern battleships without the cost.

(Above) Another 1938 view of a *Cavour*-class battleship, in company with Heavy Cruiser *Gorizia*. The ten 12.6" guns in four turrets coupled with 27 knot speed made the *Cavours* credible adversaries and a source of national pride. While dominating cruisers, their firepower was light compared to the 14" to 16" main batteries of Royal Navy BB. Flashy fleet reviews also masked the fact that Italian naval leadership had little experience.

These pre-war battleship photos all came from USN ONI files (likely from the same Regia Marina Review), forwarded to Washington by a USN Attaché in Rome.

Below, the admiral is being helped in or out of his greatcoat and sailors are in formation at the rail. Nine Cant-z 501 "Gull" seaplanes are doing a fly-by and several Fascist or Army officials are also aboard ship—looks like a ceremony in progress.

As old battleships were being reworked the Italian government authorized four new BB, the first to exceed Naval Treaty limits of total 35,000 tons displacement. In 1942 they would be the only Italian warships with radar. To tell the BB-classes apart, look for two three-gun forward turrets and one aft on the new ships as opposed to lower three-gun and upper two-gun turrets forward and aft on the older ships. The photo above dates from 1939. The BB on the left is either *Andrea Doria* or *Caio Duilio* (improved versions of the *Cavour* design). Upgrading of her upper works was incomplete. On the right is one of the new *Littorio* battleships. It's amusing how Naval Attachés always got hotel rooms with a view of the "ocean." Matching buildings, mole and cranes with aerial photos; this is Trieste.

These two photos show new *Littorio*-class battleships underway in late 1940, both probably Italian propaganda shots.[2] Note the unusually long-barreled 15" guns and the mid-ships arc of secondary armament turrets (four triple 6", twelve single 3.5" and 60 20mm anti-aircraft guns at strategic points throughout the superstructure). The photo of *Littorio* and *Vittorio Veneto* firing was likely from an exercise since the lead ship has just fired, but guns on the second BB are trained forward. War had begun and the United States was still "neutral" but I doubt a USN Attaché or ONI officer would have been allowed on a working warship with a camera. The photo below shows the large aft 15" turret turned all the way around to face near-forward along the port side of the vessel. The three barrels visible at the rear are the starboard-aft triple-gun 6" turret. Sharp eyes will make out its forward mate just even with the rear of the upper main turret.

When war began for Italy in June 1940, Mussolini thought it would be over quickly and threw his navy into the game prematurely lest he lose a share of the spoils. Only refurbished BB *Conte di Cavour* and *Gulio Cesare* were fully operational. Sisterships *Andrea Doria* and *Caio Duilio* were still working up. New Battleships *Vittorio Veneto* and *Littorio* were in training. The other larger BB, *Roma* and *Impero*, were under construction (*Impero* was never completed).

Regia Marina also fielded 19 cruisers. As long as the older battleships but noticeably narrower, they are easily identified on aerial photographs. Chief among these were the *Zara*-class heavy cruisers (*Zara, Pola, Fiume* and *Gorizia*). They were the fastest, most heavily armored ships of their type in the Mediterranean. Britain's Royal Navy had no answering cruisers in those waters. Two turrets forward and two aft was the rule and, except for one light cruiser, turrets carried two guns each. Italy also had over one hundred destroyers and torpedo boats and, perhaps more dangerous to the British, more than one hundred submarines of several designs including "coastal boats" and "ocean-going"

These pre-war ONI photos show the unusually close-spaced 8" main battery that were a recognition signature for a *Zara*-class heavy cruiser, in both cases probably *Gorizia*. Other Italian cruisers were also built with this unique gun arrangement. The British knew a lot about this class since *Gorizia* docked at Gibraltar for repairs in 1937 and was found to be 10% above her stated tonnage. A sister *Zara* heavy cruiser is in the background of the lower photo. None of the *Zara*'s survived the war.

The first weeks of war saw several sharp clashes in which the Italian Navy lost more ships than they sank. The Battle at Point Stilo demonstrated their poor air-sea coordination and the traditionally aggressive leadership of the Royal Navy. Royal Navy torpedo planes caught all six Italian battleships in Taranto Harbor the night of 11 November 1940; a location thought to be too shallow for aerial torpedoes to dive into the water and come up to "run depth." *Cavour, Littorio* and *Duilio* were sunk upright in shallow water (the latter two were soon repaired and refloated). The successful attack was carefully studied by navies all around the world and turned out to be a dress rehearsal for Pearl Harbor.

The next two photos are Taranto after the attack. Neither is dated but they have to be close to the event, both probably flown by RAF PR aircraft from Malta, perhaps from the same mission. First is the Mar Piccolo (Inner Harbor) with four DD, three CL and two CA berthed bow-on to the quays. Anchored in deeper water are two ships apparently damaged and leaking oil, though the larger ship may be turning, her propellers churning up the bottom silt to make those "smoke-like" patterns on the surface. On the right is a heavy cruiser, probably *Trento*, which was hit by a bomb. The ship on the left is a puzzle. Supposedly there were only cruisers in the Inner Harbor but that ship has the length-to-width ratio for a battleship—in this case 7.5:1 whereas the nearby cruiser is a much "leaner" 9.3:1.

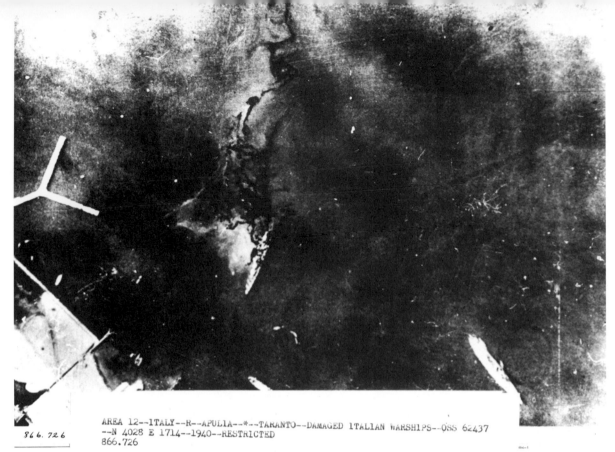

866.726

AREA 12--ITALY--R--APULIA--*--TARANTO--DAMAGED ITALIAN WARSHIPS--OSS 62437
--N 4028 E 1714--1940--RESTRICTED
866.726

The second Taranto photo (above) was taken over the Mar Grande (Outer Harbor) and shows two battleships; the one on the left leaking oil heavily and the other seemingly untouched. Again, the quality is too poor for a positive identification but the locations suggest these are *Conte di Cavour* nearest the refueling mole (the "Y" sticking out from shore) and sister-ship *Andrea Doria* at lower right.

In one night, twenty-one obsolete bi-planes (Fairey "Swordfish") from British carrier *Illustrious* cut the Italian Navy battleship force in half with far reaching results for naval balance in the Mediterranean and Axis troops in North Africa.

There followed months of small random engagements in which both sides took minor damage and the Italians lost another cruiser. Apparently nettled by poor results, the Italian Navy set out to cut off British sea-lanes to Egypt and Greece, resulting in the Battle of Cape Matapan on 27 to 29 March 1941 (the battle was actually fought over a large stretch of the Med southwest of Crete). Thinking they'd caught four British light cruisers and eight destroyers escorting a convoy, Italian Admiral Iachino led Battleship *Vittorio Veneto*, eight cruisers and 13 destroyers into battle against what turned out to be an additional four Royal Navy battleships (*Barham, Formidable, Valiant* and *Warspite*) and nine destroyers. Despite proximity to Italian airspace, no aerial reconnaissance spotted the British ships. The Royal Navy had radar, aerial recon, a carrier, and ULTRA intercepts on their side.

Surprised and under fire from radar-equipped warships in several days of running-battle, Italian sister-ships went to the aid of damaged Heavy Cruiser *Zara* and unexpectedly came under the guns of the British battleships. After the battle, the Royal Navy began to pick up survivors but had to leave the scene when Luftwaffe aircraft appeared overhead, increasing the loss of life in the rafts. The British photo caption said, "Scanty clothing proves surprise for Britain achieved." More than 2,300 Italian sailors were killed in the battle or perished in the open sea before rescue arrived.

132

Italian survivors of Cape Matapan. In an unrelated action the same day the British lost a cruiser to an Italian submarine. The Italians lost four cruisers and two destroyers. Lost also was the heart and capability for large-ship actions. Italian submarines, torpedo boats and frogmen were active and aggressive, but dominance of the sea was turning in the Mediterranean.

133

Below is a two-page Luftwaffe Recognition Sheet reflecting Italian Naval Order of Battle after the losses at Matapan and Taranto, showing *Cavour*-class but only naming the three functioning sistership. It does not anticipate operations of the twelve *Regolo*-class light cruisers scheduled for completion in 1942-43. Unfortunately it doesn't show submarines, nor did I find any photos of Italian subs in the files I searched, but they remained one of the Regia Marina's most effective weapons throughout the war, including thirty-two operating in the Atlantic out of Bordeaux, France.

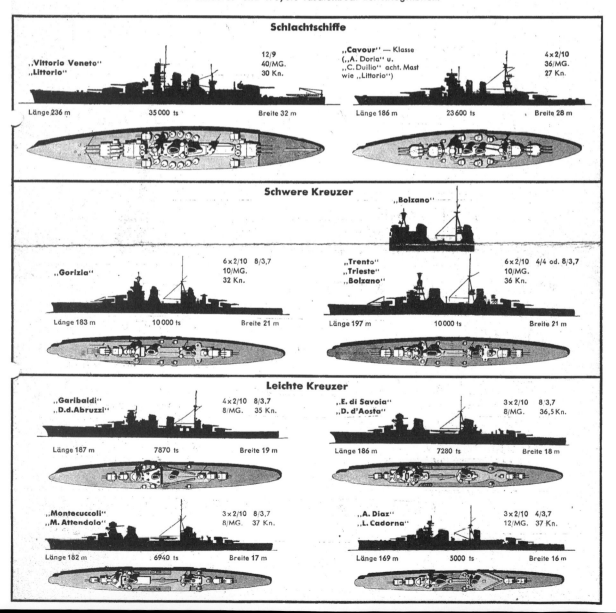

Der Oberbefehlshaber der Luftwaffe
Generalstab 5.Abtlg.

Anforderungs-Nr. **D 1210 c**

Maßstab: 1 : 2500

Neudruck
Stand: 1. Juni 1941

Italien

Kriegsschiff-Erkennungstafel

Angaben beschränken sich auf Namen des Schiffes oder der Klasse (ohne U-Boote), Flakbewaffnung (4×2 bedeutet 8 Geschütze in Doppellafette), Geschwindigkeit, Länge und Breite. Weitere Angaben siehe L.Dv. 91/3 „Die Kriegsflotten des Mittelmeeres" und Weyers Taschenbuch der Kriegsflotten.

Schlachtschiffe

„Vittorio Veneto"
„Littorio"
12/9
40/MG.
30 Kn.

„Cavour" — Klasse
(„A. Doria" u.
„C. Duilio" acht. Mast
wie „Littorio")
4×2/10
36/MG.
27 Kn.

Länge 236 m   35 000 ts   Breite 32 m   Länge 186 m   23 600 ts   Breite 28 m

Schwere Kreuzer

„Bolzano"

„Gorizia"
6×2/10 8/3,7
10/MG.
32 Kn.

„Trento"
„Trieste"
„Bolzano"
6×2/10 4/4 od. 8/3,7
10/MG.
36 Kn.

Länge 183 m   10 000 ts   Breite 21 m   Länge 197 m   10 000 ts   Breite 21 m

Leichte Kreuzer

„Garibaldi"
„D.d.Abruzzi"
4×2/10 8/3,7
8/MG. 35 Kn.

„E. di Savoia"
„D. d'Aosta"
3×2/10 8/3,7
8/MG. 36,5 Kn.

Länge 187 m   7870 ts   Breite 19 m   Länge 186 m   7280 ts   Breite 18 m

„Montecuccoli"
„M. Attendolo"
3×2/10 8/3,7
8/MG. 37 Kn.

„A. Diaz"
„L. Cadorna"
3×2/10 4/3,7
12/MG. 37 Kn.

Länge 182 m   6940 ts   Breite 17 m   Länge 169 m   5000 ts   Breite 16 m

Leichte Kreuzer

„Barbiano" — Klasse
3 x 2/10 4/3,7 12/MG. 37 Kn.
Länge 169 m   5 070 ts   Breite 16 m

„Regolo" — Klasse
3x2/6,5 14/MG. 41 Kn.
Länge 135 m   3360 ts   Breite 14 m

Kolonialkreuzer
„Eritrea"
4/3,7 2/MG. 20 Kn.
Länge 97 m   2170 ts   Breite 13 m

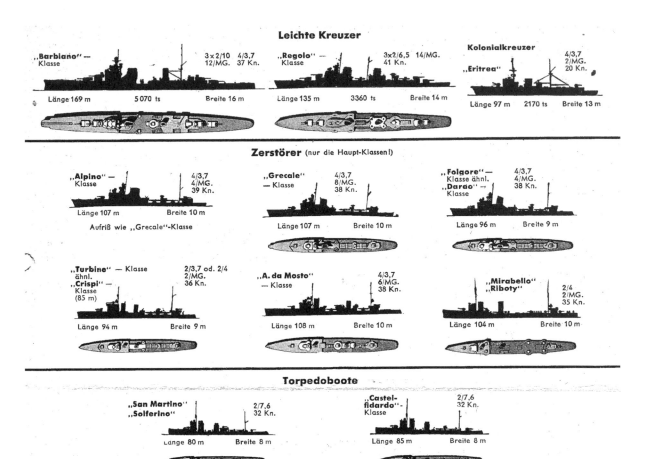

Zerstörer (nur die Haupt-Klassen!)

„Alpino" — Klasse
4/3,7 4/MG. 39 Kn.
Länge 107 m   Breite 10 m
Aufriß wie „Grecale"-Klasse

„Grecale" — Klasse
4/3,7 8/MG. 38 Kn.
Länge 107 m   Breite 10 m

„Folgore" — Klasse ähnl. **„Darao"** — Klasse
4/3,7 4/MG. 38 Kn.
Länge 96 m   Breite 9 m

„Turbine" — Klasse ähnl. **„Crispi"** — Klasse (85 m)
2/3,7 od. 2/4 2/MG. 36 Kn.
Länge 94 m   Breite 9 m

„A. da Mosto" — Klasse
4/3,7 6/MG. 38 Kn.
Länge 108 m   Breite 10 m

„Mirabello" **„Riboty"**
2/4 2/MG. 35 Kn.
Länge 104 m   Breite 10 m

Torpedoboote

„San Martino" **„Solferino"**
2/7,6 32 Kn.
Länge 80 m   Breite 8 m

„Castel-fidardo" — Klasse
2/7,6 32 Kn.
Länge 85 m   Breite 8 m

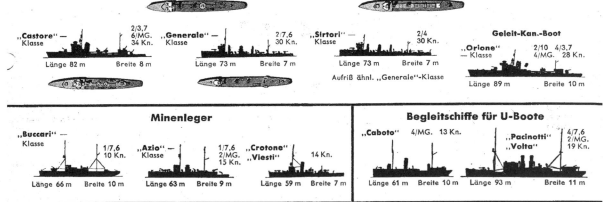

„Castore" — Klasse
2/3,7 6/MG. 34 Kn.
Länge 82 m   Breite 8 m

„Generale" — Klasse
2/7,6 30 Kn.
Länge 73 m   Breite 7 m

„Sirtori" — Klasse
2/4 30 Kn.
Länge 73 m   Breite 7 m
Aufriß ähnl. „Generale"-Klasse

Geleit-Kan.-Boot
„Orione" — Klasse
2/10 4/3,7 4/MG. 28 Kn.
Länge 89 m   Breite 10 m

Minenleger

„Buccari" — Klasse
1/7,6 10 Kn.
Länge 66 m   Breite 10 m

„Azio" — Klasse
1/7,6 2/MG. 15 Kn.
Länge 63 m   Breite 9 m

„Crotone" **„Viesti"**
14 Kn.
Länge 59 m   Breite 7 m

Begleitschiffe für U-Boote

„Caboto" 4/MG. 13 Kn.
Länge 61 m   Breite 10 m

„Pacinotti" **„Volta"**
4/7,6 2/MG. 19 Kn.
Länge 93 m   Breite 11 m

Flugzeugmutterschiff

„Giuseppe Miraglia"
4/10,2 4/MG. 21 Kn.

Länge 121 m   4880 ts   Breite 15 m

135

War in North Africa and German involvement in Russia in the spring of 1941 set the opposing British and Italian naval forces firmly at right angles to each other. Italian ships sought to supply/reinforce in Tunisia (moving north-south) while British were sending vitally needed supplies to Malta and Egypt (moving east-west) and each sought to frustrate the other's efforts but neither wanted to risk the attrition of a major engagement. German aircraft and subs were becoming more active in the region. Losses (particularly merchantmen) rose on both sides, mainly from air, submarine and light-ship actions. With only a third of the supplies sent actually reaching Tunisia, the Italian Navy took a chance with a large convoy escorted by BB *Duilio* and three cruisers supported at a distance by three other battleships and two heavy cruisers.

In a meeting-engagement with a British convoy and escorts headed for Malta in December 1941, the Italian admiral elected to protect his charges rather than engage. They all got through—which was viewed as a triumph. Another success was scored a day later when daring Italian frogmen sank Battleships *Queen Elizabeth, Valiant*, Heavy Cruiser *York* and a tanker in Alexandria harbor, further buoying Italian spirits and beginning to turn the advantage in the Mediterranean back toward the Regia Marina.

Going back to traditions begun in WW I and refined between 1935 and 1941, Italian marine-commandoes developed techniques, tactics and equipment for undersea attack (later copied by the British and U.S. Navies). The proto-frogmen were carried to Alexandria on submarines, penetrated the harbor using early versions of underwater breathing devices and riding two-man undersea mini-subs called *Maiale* ("Pig") by their crews. In Egypt they were undetected and successfully planted mines on or under the Royal Navy warships.

Gibraltar was a tougher proposition so the undersea commandoes used an old freighter moored in a Spanish port nearby as a base, slipping in and out through a hole cut in the side under water. But the British were on alert and the Alexandria success couldn't be repeated.

The upper photo shows two men riding their "pig" with a mine. The post war photo (right) shows one of the frogman vehicles in a transport cradle on what is probably a Torpedo Boat.

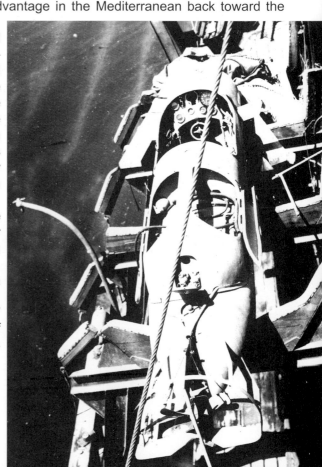

The "Battle of the Convoys" continued relentlessly through 1942 with both sides risking their warships to shepherd through crucial supplies and with both sides losing cruisers, destroyers and submarines. The RAF photo of Naples (above) on 6 January 1941 clearly demonstrates a British shift of interest from warships to merchant shipping (vessels eligible for convoys to North Africa). Since none of the annotations repeat but ship-types do, I assume the letters identified specific vessels by name, which would also identify the cargo type and volume or weight.

Note that between "J" and "G" the distinctive images of a *Littorio*-class (the larger warship) and *Cavour*-class battleship are not even annotated.

137

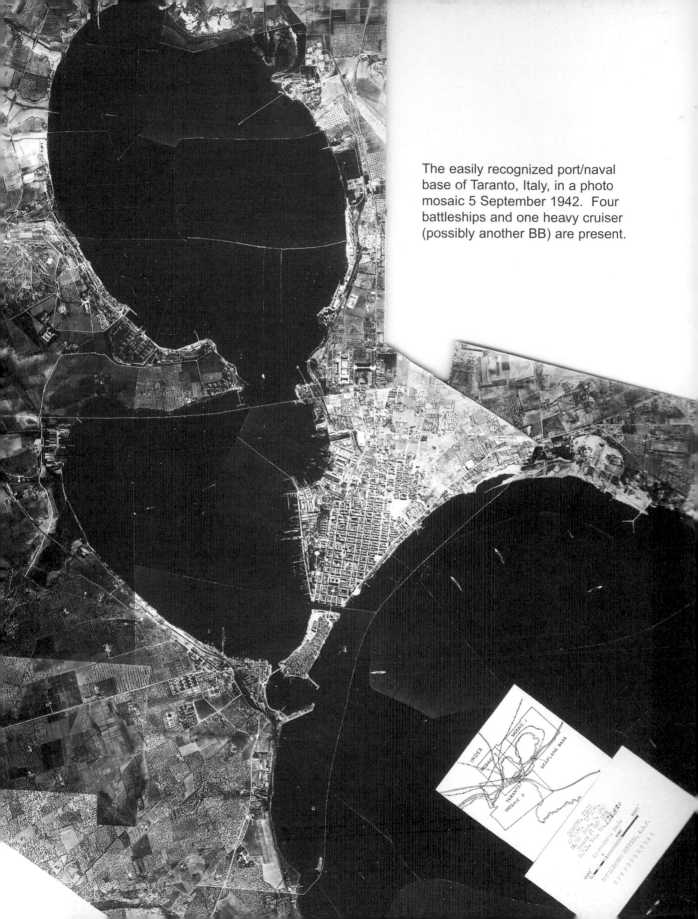

The easily recognized port/naval base of Taranto, Italy, in a photo mosaic 5 September 1942. Four battleships and one heavy cruiser (possibly another BB) are present.

The overly optimistic caption on the imagery above says: "These photographs were taken on 28.3.41 during a bombing attack on the Italian Fleet, by aircraft of the Middle East Command to assess bombing results." The position of these units is given as 35 degrees 42' N. 20 degrees 55' E. (off Kythera Island, south of Greece). "A. A possible Cruiser. B. Bolsano Cruiser modified Trento type, taking avoiding action. C. 2 bombs bursting in the water some distance from the starboard quarter of a cruiser, Condotieri or Trento type. This vessel has taken evasive action, greatly hindering the aim of the bomber crew, which otherwise might have scored a hit."

(Below) Genoa on 14 April 1941 showing numerous merchant ships, including two large tankers. A *Cavour*-class battleship is in drydock (arrow), possibly *Duilio* having Taranto damage being repaired. Note three large liners (longer than the BB) moored at moles in the inner harbor (photo top).

(Above) BB *Conte di Cavour* was still at Taranto on 27 September 1941. Refloated and guarded by double lines of anti-torpedo nets (their cork floats show as a string of pearls against the dark water). She was eventually repaired at Trieste, but never saw action again.

The Allies were very serious about watching the ships at Taranto as the photo plots from just two days in September show. Both reflect daring, relatively low (8 to 10K feet alt) multiple-pass photo runs over the port—three passes on the left plot, four on the right.

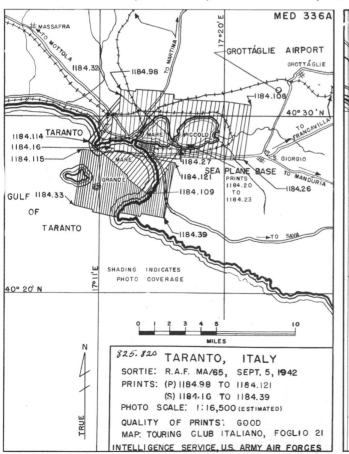

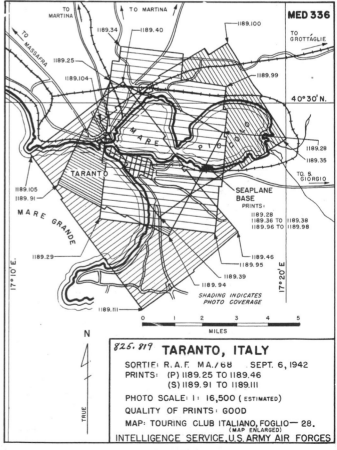

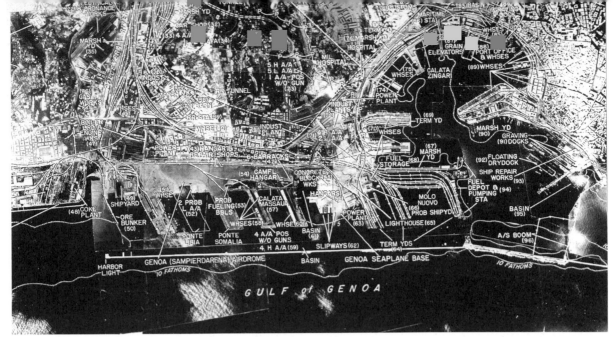

GENOA, ITALY

PHOTO INTELLIGENCE REPORT NO. 239
44° 24' N. 8° 55' E.

DATE OF PHOTOGRAPHY: JUNE 10, 1942
APPROXIMATE SCALE

1000'   0   1000'   2000'

OFFICE OF THE
ASST. C/AS, INTELLIGENCE

640.12B   PART 2

The annotated uncontrolled photo-mosaic of Genoa (above) is more evidence of a shift in interest by Intelligence from Naval Order of Battle to bombing targets and defenses. A probable heavy cruiser in the Floating Drydock (annotation 92) isn't even mentioned.

Emphasis change is also shown in a detailed photo interpretation analysis of La Spezia. The uncontrolled mosaic below uses September 1942 imagery but probably dates from early 1943. All the defenses and facilities are meticulously identified and the only mobile targets noted are seaplanes moored off shore. This is a report produced to support targeting for the growing power of RAF and 15th Air Force bombers flying out of North Africa after the Allied invasion of North Africa (Operation Torch) in November 1942. It underlines that the offensive threat presented by the Italian navy was almost negligible.

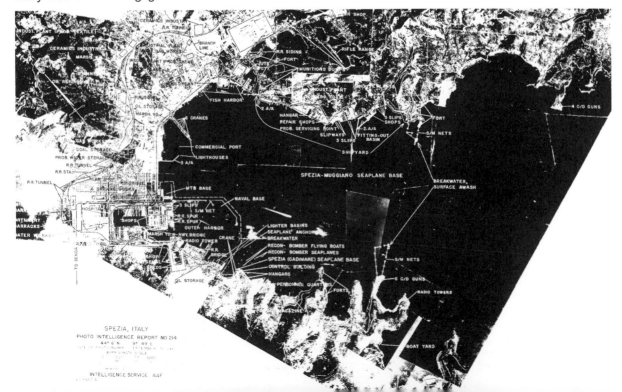

SPEZIA, ITALY
PHOTO INTELLIGENCE REPORT NO 214
44° 6' N   9° 49' E

INTELLIGENCE SERVICE, AAF

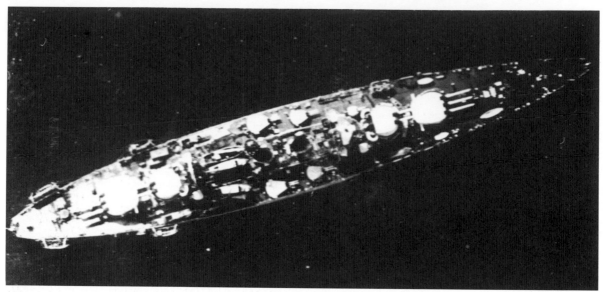

(Above) A good look at the four 4.7" twin secondary batteries in wedge-shaped turrets on a *Cavour*-class BB, 1942, probably at Trieste. Sources cite six twin 4.7" turrets—if so, the two aft-most are under something (see Luftwaffe Recognition Guide for location).

A PI Report on Genoa (below) using 9 November 1942 imagery, emphasized shipbuilding and port facilities. Only three of the twelve *Regolo* light cruisers were completed.

INTERPRETATION REPORT Nº S.15
Photograph 3
TRIESTE
C/730 — 23·12·42 — PHOTO 56(36)
(A) Hull of battleship "Impero" showing clearly (1) the barbettes of the main armament, two temporarily covered. (2) the funnel uptakes, and (3) the light A.A. positions mounted temporarily
(B) The Battleship "Conte di Cavour", repairs almost completed after being damaged at Taranto in November 1940.
(C) 210' Escort Vessels fitting out. Note also on the quay, (4) 3 guns, probably 15", (5) Parts of turrets, all but one screened by a temporary cover.

801.583
Neg.No. 2066.

Imagery of 23 December 1942 covered the shipyards at Trieste with BB *Cavour* and the fourth *Littorio*-class BB, *Impero*, under construction. Neither vessel was operational before the war ended. That "fuzzy" look around *Cavour* is apparently netting intended to disrupt the hull outline and confuse reconnaissance—if so, typical of most camouflage, it wouldn't fool a PI (in any case, the Allies weren't bombing as far north as Trieste until the spring of 1944). Torpedo nets protected both ships. One has to admire the skill of the PIs who could identify "parts of turrets" on the quay (and under cover no less), but then they had recently seen the same thing with the German Battlecruiser *Gneisenau* at Gdynia, Poland.

143

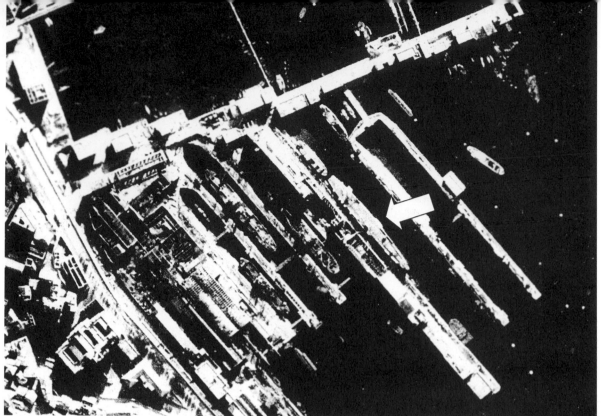

Meanwhile, in Genoa, on 21 December 1942 (above and right), the hull of pre-war liner *Roma* was well on the way to conversion to an aircraft carrier. The Italian Navy didn't have a CV and Taranto had certainly proven their value, so conversion of an existing hull (the liner *Roma*) was the fastest building alternative. Regia Marina had already assigned the name *Roma* to a BB so the conversion was renamed *Aquila* (Eagle). Like the German effort, it was questionable from the start and a great deal of wishful thinking. If they could have made the ship operational, how would they have fielded an air component with no training and no aircraft designed for carrier take-off and landing? There is often a considerable gap between knowing what you want to do and doing it.

(Right) Photo Interpreters sometimes make mistakes. Using the 21 December 1942 imagery, Intelligence reported that the carrier was based upon a *Regolo*-class Light Cruiser hull, probably a result of seeing one in this location on 9 November (see photo on page 142).

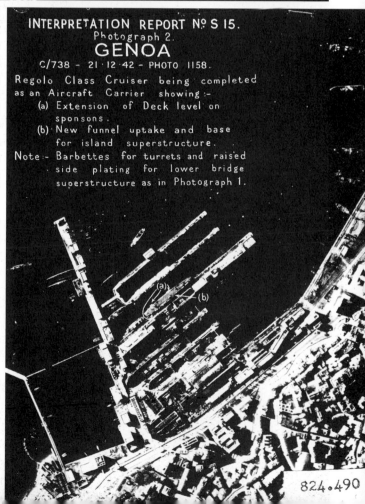

INTERPRETATION REPORT N? S 15.
Photograph 2.
GENOA
C/738 - 21·12·42 - PHOTO 1158.
Regolo Class Cruiser being completed as an Aircraft Carrier showing :-
(a) Extension of Deck level on sponsons.
(b) New funnel uptake and base for island superstructure.
Note :- Barbettes for turrets and raised side plating for lower bridge superstructure as in Photograph 1.

824·490

SPEZIA, ITALY

La Spezia Harbor, 5 June 1943. This time the photo was from a B-17 of the 99th Bomb Group out of North Africa flying at 23,000 feet. The target was "shipping." Aside from a few strays, most of the bombs are near the biggest ship in port, a *Littorio*-class battleship. Close, but no cigar.

Moments later another bomber dropped on a large ship near the harbor entrance (arrow). Churned water near *Littorio* (upper left) is settling and new bombs are near another large ship (possibly a *Cavour* BB) moored along the breakwater. A CA is moored near *Littorio*.

On 2 July 1943 the carrier-conversion was moved to another part of Genoa Harbor. A *Littorio*-class battleship is near the floating drydock—two turrets forward, one aft.

The Italian Navy was being hunted down in every port it used. Below, Messina, 31 January 1943. A large merchant ship, three CL and several DD were 15th Air Force 98th BG targets.

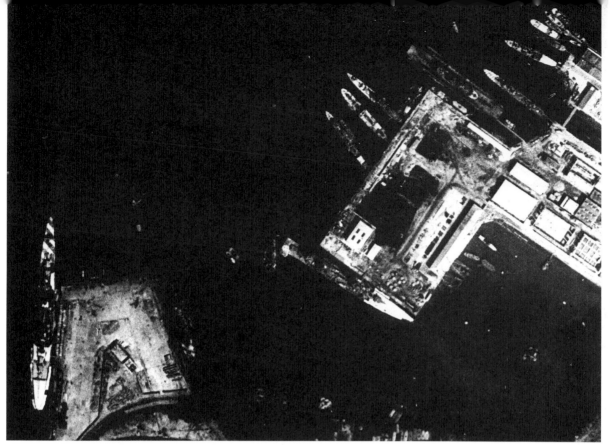

(Above) Recon of Messina on an earlier date caught a heavy cruiser in port (far left). A light cruiser is at photo center, possibly one of the *Regolos*.

(Below) BBs *Cavour* (left) and *Impero* were still in work. Trieste, 21 January 1944.

Finally, lack of fuel began to curtail Italian sorties and introduction of American air and naval forces began to slowly swing the advantage firmly to the Allies—where it remained. Anything the Italian Navy might have done was moot after May 1943 with the fall of North Africa and the Allied invasion of Sicily in June.

Following Italian surrender to the Allies on 8 September 1943, Battleships *Roma, Vittorio Veneto* and *Littorio*, three cruisers and eight destroyers based at La Spezia attempted to sail to Sardinia and Malta for internment. This impromptu fle et was attacked by the Luftwaffe. At left, flagship *Roma*, Italy's most modern BB, was sunk by the first operational use of "smart bombs" (FX-1400), going down with all hands including the Fleet Commander. The remaining vessels reached Malta and some (Italian cruisers and smaller ships) served with the Allied navies. Other ships remaining in Italy were taken-over or destroyed by the Germans.

Since 10 April 1943, CA *Gorizia* had been at Spezia to repair bomb damage. The photo below is from 6 February 1944. Other ships are the 1908 *Dreadnought*-style cruiser *San Marco*; now a target ship (circles on the deck fore and aft used to be barbettes) and a freight-passenger ship (note numerous lifeboats, booms and open hold). *Gorizia* is the bottom ship.

(Below) An enlargement of 14 May 1944 RAF 683Sq. reconnaissance imagery of Genoa Harbor showing carrier *Aquila*. Many of the needed modifications for operations were clearly finished and shadow shows the shape of the new superstructure. Shadows also show the lowered close-spaced plane elevators near the island.

The low altitude oblique above was taken on 15 July 1945, probably by the OSS after U.S. occupation of Genoa. Look past the collier sunk as a blockship and over the mole with all the fuel tanks—there is *Aquila* facing you, turned 180 degrees since the 14 May photo. After the Italians switched sides, Germans took control of the ship. It was damaged by Allied bombing in June 1944 and Italian commando frogmen scuttled her in shallow water beside the quay on 19 April 1945 to keep the Germans from using *Aquila* as a blockship.

Another of the 15 July 1945 obliques at Genoa.

A ground shot of *Aquila* taken shortly after U.S. troops entered Genoa at the end of April 1945.

Below, Just beyond the men in the boat is the anti-torpedo bulge added to the liner's hull to make it more war-worthy. That feature would normally be below the water-line. At this point *Aquila* would seem to be sitting on the bottom. Note camouflage netting still in place.

CA *Bolzano* and damaged Spezia harbor facilities, 19 April 45 (above). It would be satisfying to attribute that damage to Allied aerial bombing but most of it was probably German ground demolition like damage at the Italian port of Tripoli in January 1943 (at right).

(Below) Taranto 18 May 1945. One of the surviving BB, probably *Caio Duilio*. The tall ship just behind the mole at right is probably *Amerigo Vespucci*. (Thanks to World Naval Ship Forum for helping ID this location)

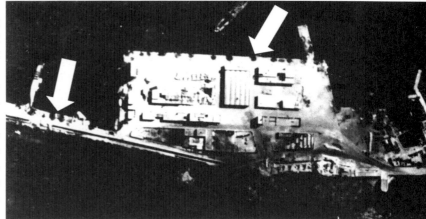

(Above) Trieste on 18 May 1945 showing what is probably BB *Conte di Cavour*, a heavy cruiser, two light cruisers and several DD interned after the war. The full-rigged ship is *Cristoforo Colombo*. For some reason the fourth narrow footbridge from the mole to the ships is packed with men watching something—perhaps the aircraft taking the photo.

Sad end for a proud naval greyhound. Probably CA *Gorizia* at La Spezia—no date specified but certainly after June 1944.

FOOTNOTES

[1]Rebuilt *Cavour*'s had 3,000 mile range where Royal Navy *King George V* BB could cruise 14,000 miles.

[2]The ONI caption gives a date of 1941, but, that is probably an acquisition date for the photo file. Both the new BB could have been at sea together from May to 11 November 1940, then not again until after September 1941.

PLACES MENTIONED IN CHAPTER IV

153

CHAPTER V
MARINE NATIONALE
THE AXIS FLEET THAT MIGHT HAVE BEEN

Luftwaffe Recognition Sheets (below) show the French Fleet just before war began in the west. A Fleet in being is a potential threat to everyone else and an uncommitted French Navy threatened both sides.

Der Oberbefehlshaber der Luftwaffe
Generalstab 5. Abtlg.

Anforderungs-Nr. **D 1210 b**

Maßstab: 1:2500
(soweit nicht anders angegeben)

Stand: April 1940

Frankreich
Erkennungstafel

Angaben beschränken sich auf Namen des Schiffes oder der Klasse (ohne U-Boote), Flakbewaffnung (4x2 bedeutet 8 Geschütze in Doppellafette), Geschwindigkeit, Länge und Breite. Weitere Angaben siehe L. Dv. 91/3 und Weyers Taschenbuch der Kriegsflotten. Die hinter der Klasse eingeklammerte Zahl gibt an, wieviel Schiffe zu der Klasse gehören.

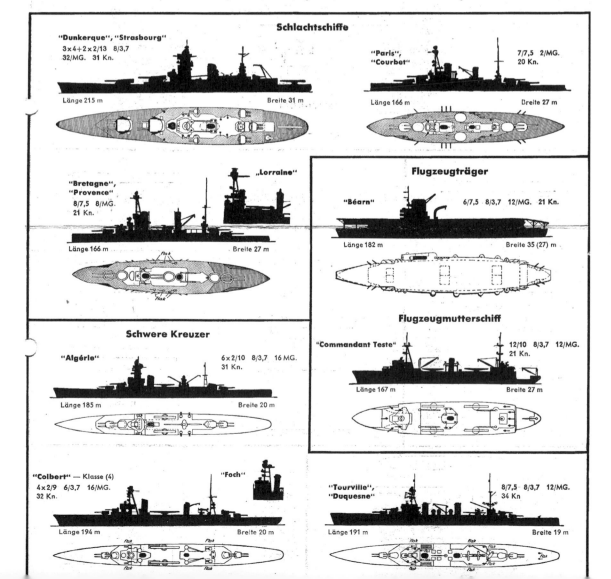

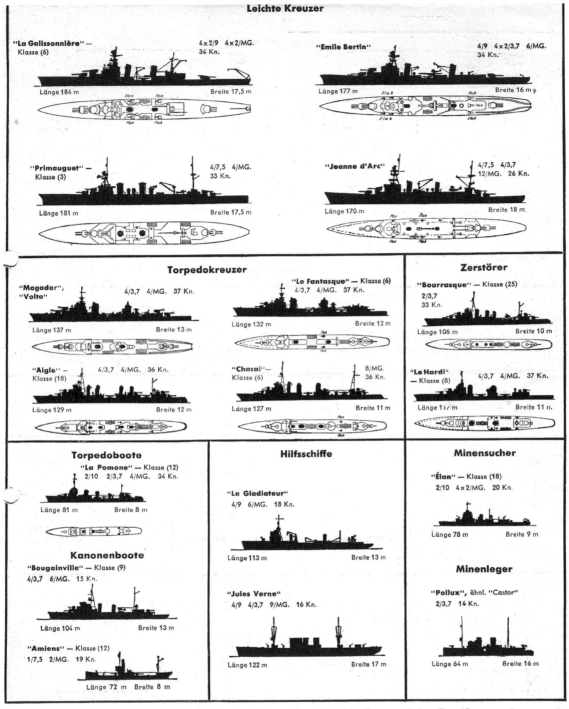

Leichte Kreuzer

"La Galissonnière" — Klasse (6) — 4 x 2/9 4 x 2/MG. 34 Kn.
Länge 184 m Breite 17,5 m

"Emile Bertin" — 4/9 4 x 2/3,7 6/MG. 34 Kn.
Länge 177 m Breite 16 m

"Primauguet" — Klasse (3) — 4/7,5 4/MG. 33 Kn.
Länge 181 m Breite 17,5 m

"Jeanne d'Arc" — 4/7,5 4/3,7 12/MG. 26 Kn.
Länge 170 m Breite 18 m

Torpedokreuzer

"Mogador", "Volta" — 4/3,7 4/MG. 37 Kn.
Länge 137 m Breite 13 m

"Le Fantasque" — Klasse (6) — 4/3,7 4/MG. 37 Kn.
Länge 132 m Breite 12 m

"Aigle" — Klasse (18) — 4/3,7 4/MG. 36 Kn.
Länge 129 m Breite 12 m

"Chacal" — Klasse (6) — 8/MG. 36 Kn.
Länge 127 m Breite 11 m

Zerstörer

"Bourrasque" — Klasse (25) — 2/3,7 33 Kn.
Länge 106 m Breite 10 m

"Le Hardi" — Klasse (8) — 4/3,7 4/MG. 37 Kn.
Länge 117 m Breite 11 m

Torpedoboote

"La Pomone" — Klasse (12) — 2/10 2/3,7 4/MG. 34 Kn.
Länge 81 m Breite 8 m

Kanonenboote

"Bougainville" — Klasse (9) — 4/3,7 6/MG. 15 Kn.
Länge 104 m Breite 13 m

"Amiens" — Klasse (12) — 1/7,5 2/MG. 19 Kn.
Länge 72 m Breite 8 m

Hilfsschiffe

"Le Gladiateur" — 4/9 6/MG. 18 Kn.
Länge 113 m Breite 13 m

"Jules Verne" — 4/9 4/3,7 9/MG. 16 Kn.
Länge 122 m Breite 17 m

Minensucher

"Élan" — Klasse (18) — 2/10 4 x 2/MG. 20 Kn.
Länge 78 m Breite 9 m

Minenleger

"Pollux", ähnl. "Castor" — 2/3,7 14 Kn.
Länge 64 m Breite 16 m

France was a global power with colonies in Africa, the West Indies and the Pacific, so she needed a fleet to "show the flag" and maintain lines of communication to those possessions as well as defend the homeland. She also had Naval Ports in the Mediterranean and on the Atlantic that the Germans wanted to use. The French Navy was well balanced in ship types though limited by finances. There were relatively few modern vessels—but those were of innovative design: fast and powerful. They were not intended to face the Royal Navy, rather mainly pointed at countering the fast Italian battleships and cruisers and, to a lesser extent, German warships. Fast, heavily armed destroyers

155

were a match for light cruisers in other fleets. The impressive Heavy Cruiser *Algérie* was a direct response to Italy's *Zara*-class cruisers and "Fast Battleships" *Dunkerque* and *Strasbourg* were intended to answer the German pocket-battleships with more armor, firepower and speed. These were important ships in capability and with numbers that might sway the naval balance of power in any theater of operations. Some had proven themselves helping the Royal Navy hunt down *Graf Spee* in 1939; others were involved in operations off Norway and defending sea-lanes in the Mediterranean and Atlantic.

Pre-war photos of new "Fast Battleship" *Dunkerque* (above accompanied by WW I-era Battleships *Provence* and *Lorraine*). All main guns forward in two large turrets significantly reduced weight and that made for speed within Treaty limits. In 1936-37 the 31 knot BB with eight 11" guns was more than a match for Germany's latest offerings.

A football field longer and only one knot slower, BB *Richelieu* was armed with main batteries of 15" guns in the same two-turret arrangement as the earlier "Fast Battleships." Commissioned in July 1940, just in time for the war, her natural foes would have been *Bismarck* and Italy's *Littorio*-class battleships, but action on the ground obviated those match-ups. The ship never got a chance to show what she could do. The photos on this page were probably collected by a U.S. Naval Attaché as *Richelieu* was working up in early 1940.

With German troops sweeping into France in June 1940, some French ships fled to British, neutral or French Colonial ports. For example, France's only aircraft carrier, *Bearn*, put in to Martinique in the West Indies. Others went to ports in the south of France or sought to remain outside direct Nazi control in French North African ports (Casablanca and Oran). The French Navy could, and would, fight for the honor of France, but they had little sympathy or enthusiasm for the Fascist Vichy regime.

The puppet Vichy government gave hope that French warships would remain under French control and idle but there was no guarantee that the arrangement would last. In particular, control of the Mediterranean was at hazard. Offers to French ships to join the Royal Navy fighting the Germans or disarm were declined as likely to incite German retaliation in Occupied France. Britain's back was against the wall. It was only a month since the Dunkirk evacuation, German soldiers and airmen were massing in English Channel Ports 22 miles away. The risk of having so many fine warships added to forces arrayed against them was too great Britain. The result was a 3 July 1940 Royal Navy surprise attack (Operation Catapult) on the largest collection of French warships outside the Luftwaffe umbrella; those at the port of Mers-el-Kebir (Oran) in western Algeria.

The old Battleship *Bretagne* was destroyed. Old BB *Provence*, modern BB *Dunkerque* and DD *Mogador* were damaged and run aground to keep them from sinking. Aside from the loss of warships, the death of 1,297 of their sailors at the hands of their recent ally was particularly galling for the French.

Battleship *Bretagne* hit and sinking at Mers-el Kebir, Algeria, 3 July 1940.

157

(Above) Another shot of *Bretagne*, obviously taken from another French warship and probably picked up by a U.S. Naval Attaché, winding up in ONI Archives in Washington.

(Below) Old BBs *Bretagne* and *Provence* under fire early in the attack.

(Above) The once magnificent Heavy Cruiser *Algérie* sunk at her mooring.

(Below) "Fast Battleship" *Strasbourg* being hit. One has to admire the determination of the photographer continuing to take photos with all that going on around him.

Above, BB *Dunkerque* was sunk in shallow water with serious hull damage.

Despite hard feelings and tension between British and French resulting from the attack, five days later French naval units in Alexandria, Egypt, agreed to disarm for the duration. The following day Royal Navy aircraft disabled modern BB *Richelieu* at Dakar, Senegal. That left the bulk of active French naval vessels in Toulon Harbor, forty miles southeast of Marseille. French retaliation for "Catapult" was to ineffectively bomb Gibraltar from bases in Algeria on 24 and 25 September 1940. Year-end saw the Luftwaffe summarizing the disposition of French warships in two camps as below.

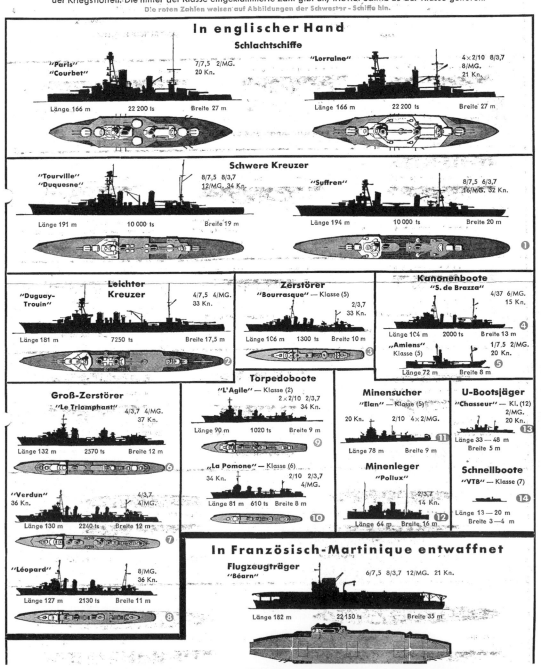

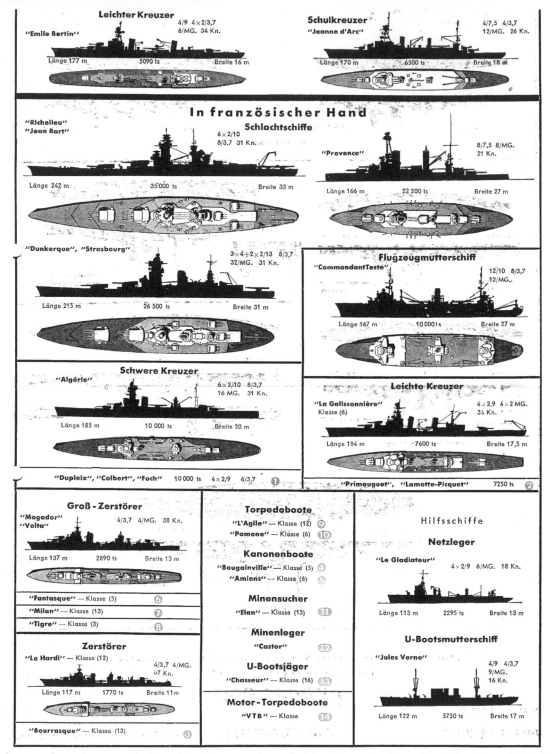

Leichter Kreuzer

"Emile Bertin" 4/9 4×2/3,7 6/MG. 34 Kn.
Länge 177 m 5090 ts Breite 16 m

Schulkreuzer

"Jeanne d'Arc" 4/7,5 4/3,7 12/MG. 26 Kn.
Länge 170 m 6500 ts Breite 18 m

In französischer Hand

Schlachtschiffe

"Richelieu" "Jean Bart" 6×2/10 8/3,7 31 Kn.
Länge 242 m 35 000 ts Breite 33 m

"Provence" 8/7,5 8/MG. 21 Kn.
Länge 166 m 22 200 ts Breite 27 m

"Dunkerque", "Strasbourg" 3×4+2×2/13 8/3,7 32/MG. 31 Kn.
Länge 215 m 26 500 ts Breite 31 m

Flugzeugmutterschiff

"CommandantTeste" 12/10 8/3,7 12/MG.
Länge 167 m 10 000 ts Breite 27 m

Schwere Kreuzer

"Algérie" 6×2/10 8/3,7 16 MG. 31 Kn.
Länge 185 m 10 000 ts Breite 20 m

Leichte Kreuzer

"La Galissonnière" Klasse (6) 4×2,9 4×2 MG. 34 Kn.
Länge 184 m 7600 ts Breite 17,5 m

"Dupleix", "Colbert", "Foch" 10 000 ts 4×2/9 6/3,7 ①

"Primauguet", "Lamotte-Picquet" 7250 ts ②

Groß - Zerstörer

"Mogador" "Volta" 4/3,7 4/MG. 38 Kn.
Länge 137 m 2890 ts Breite 13 m

"Fantasque" — Klasse (5) ⑥
"Milan" — Klasse (13) ⑦
"Tigre" — Klasse (3) ⑧

Zerstörer

"Le Hardi" — Klasse (12) 4/3,7 4/MG. 37 Kn.
Länge 117 m 1770 ts Breite 11m

"Bourrasque" — Klasse (13) ③

Torpedoboote

"L'Agile" — Klasse (12) ⑨
"Pomone" — Klasse (6) ⑩

Kanonenboote

"Bougainville" — Klasse (5) ④
"Amiens" — Klasse (6) ⑤

Minensucher

"Elan" — Klasse (13) ⑪

Minenleger

"Castor" ⑫

U-Bootsjäger

"Chasseur" — Klasse (16) ⑬

Motor-Torpedoboote

"VTB" — Klasse ⑭

Hilfsschiffe

Netzleger

"Le Gladiateur" 4×2/9 6/MG. 18 Kn.
Länge 113 m 2295 ts Breite 13 m

U-Bootsmutterschiff

"Jules Verne" 4/9 4/3,7 9/MG. 16 Kn.
Länge 122 m 5750 ts Breite 17 m

White numbers in gray circles show the number of ships in each class (e.g., fourteen VTB Motor-Torpedo boats). With 5.4" guns, the "heavy destroyers" were almost light cruisers and the 45 knot *Fantasque*-class were the fastest DD ever built. Unfinished large Battleship *Jean Bart*, sistership of *Richelieu*, had fled to Casablanca ahead of the German advance and was not attacked during

162

Operation Catapult because it wasn't considered a threat. The photos below were probably taken by ONI agents and date from before the U.S. was in the war. Only one turret is armed and none of the aft secondary batteries have been installed. (Rick's Café Américain is somewhere off to the right.)

In January 1941, *Strasbourg* was moored at Mers-el-Kebir inside a double fence of anti-torpedo nets, below. She looks operational.

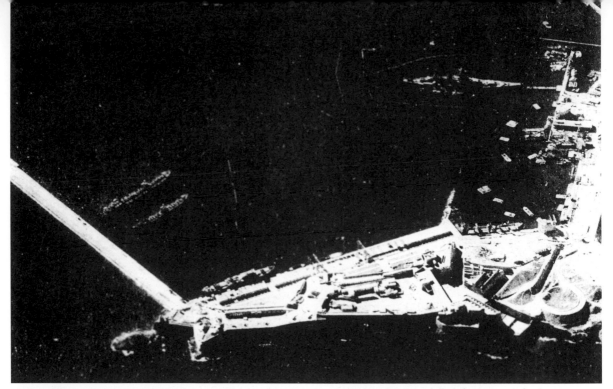

(Above) Another view *Strasbourg*. Mers-el-Kebir, French Algeria, 19 January 1941.

(Below) *Richelieu* at Dakar, Senegal, 3 November 1942. After Operation Catapult, frequent British recon flights between South Africa and Gibraltar kept a close watch on this damaged but still formidable warship. The upper main turret is turned to look back to sea over her portside.

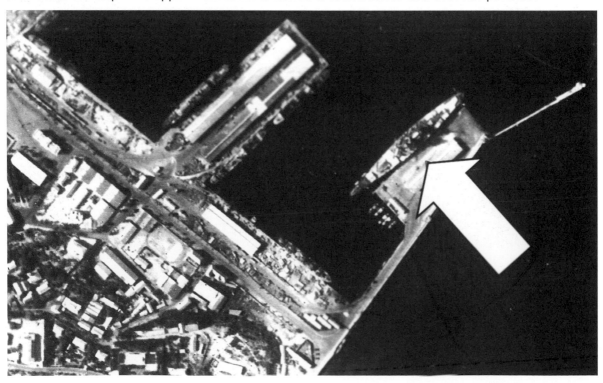

Enlargement of excellent imagery from 26 November 1942 shows *Richelieu* inside torpedo nets at Dakar. A 15" gun in her upper turret is missing. Aerial torpedo damage from a British attack on 23 July 1940 doesn't show, but it made the ship "a fixed defense" facility for Dakar since hull repair was impossible there. Main battery damage was caused by "blow-back" from one of her own guns, disabling two barrels during a 24 September duel with Battleship HMS *Barham*. Only two gangways from the mole suggests limited activity.

(Below) The world's largest submarine, *Surcouf*, fled to Portsmouth, UK ahead of the Germans in 1940 and joined the Free French cause. She sank mysteriously (probably from collision with a freighter) near Panama on 18 February 1942. One of a kind, *Surcouf* had ten torpedo tubes, twin 8" guns, four 13.2mm and two 37mm AA guns and carried a motorboat and airplane. These photos are from a 1940 German study of French and English navies.

A PI Report on Toulon Harbor using 10 June 1942 imagery. Warships are moored at annotation 47 with "Fast Battleship" *Strasbourg* on the left, Heavy Cruiser *Algérie* next, another CA and three CL further to the right. BB *Dunkerque* is beside the mole below annotation 38. Another CA is in Missiessy Basin, there are CL near annotation 32, and several DD at annotations 12, 36 and 39.

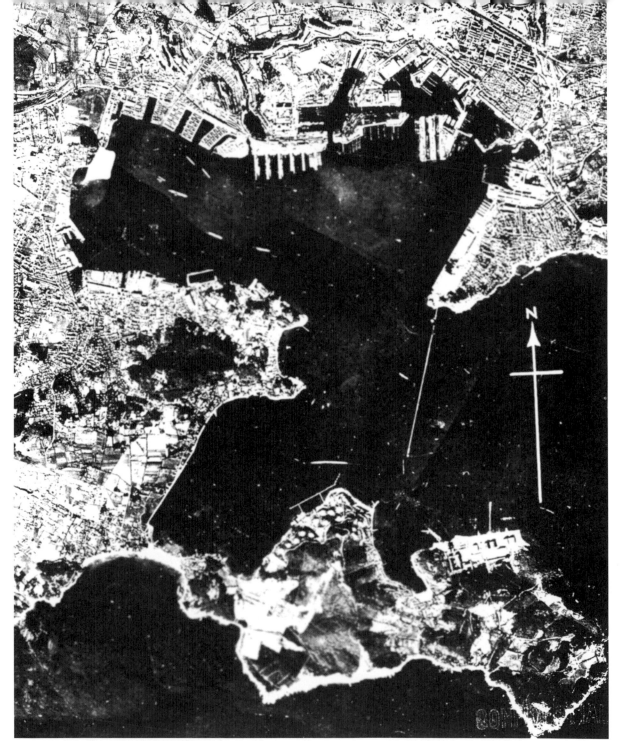

Above is a photo mosaic typical of the type of comprehensive coverage the Allies were collecting in frequent aerial reconnaissance flights over Toulon. This was part of a program to gather intelligence for the invasion of southern France as well as to watch the potentially dangerous warships. The French Fleet at Toulon was still a valuable card in the game; coveted by the Americans, British, Free French, Vichy French and Germans.

167

Seventeen months after Operation Catapult, on 8 Nov 42, Operation Torch put Allied troops ashore at several locations in French North Africa, partly with a help of a secret deal cut with commander of Vichy forces in North Africa, Admiral Darlan, which would give him control of the French Navy in return for his support. At Casablanca, still incomplete Battleship *Jean Bart* resisted and was damaged in a duel with USN BB *Massachusetts* and carrier planes from USS *Ranger*, resulting in her grounding to avoid sinking. Torch provided an excuse (or motivation) for other French warships to go over to the Allies.

When the Germans learned of Darlan's secret arrangement they swept away the puppet French government and began to occupy Vichy France (the southeastern portion of the country), also moving to take control of French ships within their grasp at Toulon.

On 27 November, in a brave act of defiance, French sailors scuttled their vessels rather than turn them over to German soldiers who were at that moment entering the Toulon Naval Base. Sunk or burned beside their berthing moles were Battleships *Strasbourg*, *Dunkerque*, and *Provence*; Heavy Cruisers *Algérie*, *Dupleix*, *Foch*, and *Colbert*; Light Cruisers *La Galissonnière*, *Marseillaise*, and *Jean de Vienne* (in drydock); Seaplane Tender *Commandant Teste*; 16 destroyers, 13 torpedo-boats; 16 submarines; and eight or ten other small warships.

RAF photoreconnaissance recorded the results on 28 November. The heavy smoke at lower left is from *Algérie* and another heavy cruiser close to photo-center. Note Destroyer hulls just showing above water along the Coal Depot Island. The "Fast Battleships" (arrows) are in a drydock at lower right and next to burning *Algérie* at lower left.

Underlining the importance of this event to the Allies, as soon as they got word of it an RAF Spitfire was dispatched from England to get photos to London as fast as possible. I'm sure the photo lab and PI shop at Medmenham (ACIU) worked "flat-out" to get results to Allied leaders the next morning. One can imagine the enormous Allied jubilation that those French warships had been "taken off the table" and were no longer a potential threat.

(Above) Mers-el-Kebir survivor *Strasbourg* appears down at the bow and neighbor *Algérie* is burning for almost her entire length, her smoke making it hard to assess damage to other ships moored nearby. At least three DDs are on their sides (upper right).

Note that the merchant or support ships (including two large tankers) anchored in deeper water didn't participate in the act of defiance.

169

(Above) Another Oran survivor (photo from Mers-el-Kebir), sea plane tender *Commandant Teste* was scuttled at Toulon.

(Above) A German officer looks at scuttled Motor-Torpedo Boats.

(Left) Another ground photo from a post-war civilian German publication correctly says an explosion on *Strasbourg* began the affair and claims the photo shows ships still burning two days later. This ship is one of the *Suffren*-class heavy cruisers (*Colbert, Dupleix* or *Foch*).

Der 29. November 1942

Als am 29. November um 3 Uhr morgens deutsche Flieger über dem Hafen und deutsche Panzer in den Straßen von Toulon erschienen, erschütterte eine Reihe von Explosionen, die erste auf dem Schlachtschiff „Strasbourg", die Stadt.

170

Schlachtschiff „Strasbourg"

In einer am 29. November veröffentlichten Erklärung der Vichy-Regierung wurde die Selbstzerstörung der französischen Flotte auf die Ausführung alter, noch aus der Zeit der Waffenstillstandsverhandlungen stammender Befehle zurückgeführt. Eine sie verhindernde Einschaltung höherer Stellen sei durch die Schnelligkeit des unerwarteten deutschen Vorgehens gegen Toulon unmöglich gemacht worden. — Die schwerbeschädigte „Strasbourg" (26 500 Tonnen) nach ihrer Hebung.

(Above) Another contemporary German ground photo of *Strasbourg* afloat but minus her foretop. The background ship with the large flying bridge is *Commandant Teste*. We know from aerial photos that no other ships were, or could be, moored/sunk near her like this at Toulon so this photo may actually be from Oran. Two of the guns are missing from the lower main turret.

(Left) The enlagement of a 28 November 1942 vertical shows *Algérie* on fire and *Strasbourg* reportedly "down at the bow." She shows some apparent fire damage amidships but all main guns are in place, making the ground photo above more of an enigma.

The float plane at lower left is probably a German Arado Ar 196.

The Allies continued to watch French ships being slowly raised and repaired but it was clear none would be seaworthy again for a long time. The hastily made mosaic above is from 13 March 1943. Referring to annotations on the 10 June 42 graphic (ten photos back), DDs at "12" are still under water. It appears *Dunkerque* is back in the Graving Dock at annotation "37." *Dunkerque*, *Commandant Teste* and old BB *Bretagne* or *Provence* are at annotation "40.". *Strasbourg* and *Algérie* haven't moved but the CA seems to have her deck above water. The port is eerily inactive.

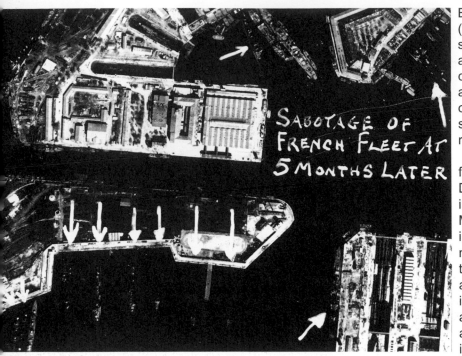

Better imagery of 5 April 1943 (left) shows ships still sunk or seriously damaged (contemporary arrow annotations). A heavy cruiser is apparently doing better at top center and the stern of one of the "Fast Battleships" is just showing in the drydock at lower right.

The annotated photo below is from a 17 March 44 PI Bomb Damage Report, using 14 March imagery to analyze an attack of 11 March. Numbers indicate individual bomb hits, though numerous impacts (more than thirty) on the "Coal Depot Island" are unmarked. Without the report it is hard to tell what the other annotations mean but the 1s, 7s and 8s are all stand-alone bomb impacts—perhaps marking the location of "strays" (it looks like they missed counting several). Newly sunk ships seem to be the meaning of annotations 2 and 4. Damaged facilities/buildings may account for annotations 5 and 6.

Identifying the major ships is easier. Starting at lower left, *Strasbourg* and *Algérie* (still sunk) are their original positions. Moving right, between moles 5 and 6 are the old BB *Provence* and *Bretagne*. Above annotation 1, the cruiser moored alongside the "Graving Dock Island" on 5 April 43 appears to have capsized and is leaning against the mole. "Fast Battleship" *Dunkerque* is still in the drydock.

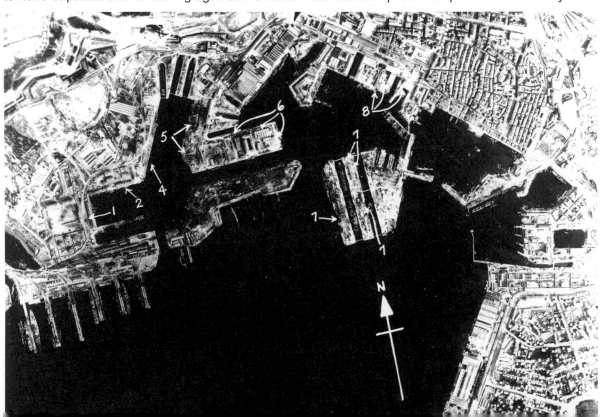

In an interesting aside to the Toulon scuttlings, a German Naval Intelligence analyst meticulously kept up-dating his copy of a 1940 Warship Study (which came into Allied hands toward the end of the war), penciling in a notation for both large destroyers, *Volta* (pictured) and *Mogador*, saying "Toulon sunk." Printed footnote 1 indicated that *Mogador* was heavily damaged at Oran (Mers-el-Kebir).

Französische Groß-Zerstörer (Flottillenführer)

*Groß-Zerstörer „**Volta**" (Schwesterschiff „**Mogador**"¹)), 2884 ts, 37 Kn, 137 m lang, 12,6 m breit.*
K e n n u n g : 2 weit auseinanderstehende Schornsteine mit kleiner Schrägkappe. Hinter dem achteren Schornstein Aufbau eines Entfernungsmessers.

Lesser damaged warships were repaired but by the time most of them were operational again the war had taken other turns and German interference was no longer a threat. In Operation Dragoon, the Allies invaded southern France on 15 August 1944. Toulon and the French ships were in Allied hands thirteen days later. Some major units of the French Navy had retained their status as a valuable asset (threat) while adroitly avoiding becoming operational under Fascist command. Refloated *Strasbourg* was sunk again by U.S. aircraft during Operation Dragoon.

Ships that went over to the Free French supported Allied landings in southern France and Normandy. Others, including the repaired and up-graded BB *Richelieu*, were active with Allied fleets from November 1943 to March 1944, then in the Far East through Japan's surrender. Based at Trincomalee after May 1944, she participated in the liberation of Singapore and reestablishment of French rule in Indochina.

Richelieu at Ceylon, 1945.

   (Below) Trincomalee, Ceylon in 1945. *Richelieu* is probably down there with the CVE and two CV, at least two BB and several CA, but the big gun ships all have canvass awnings rigged and I can't tell which she might be.

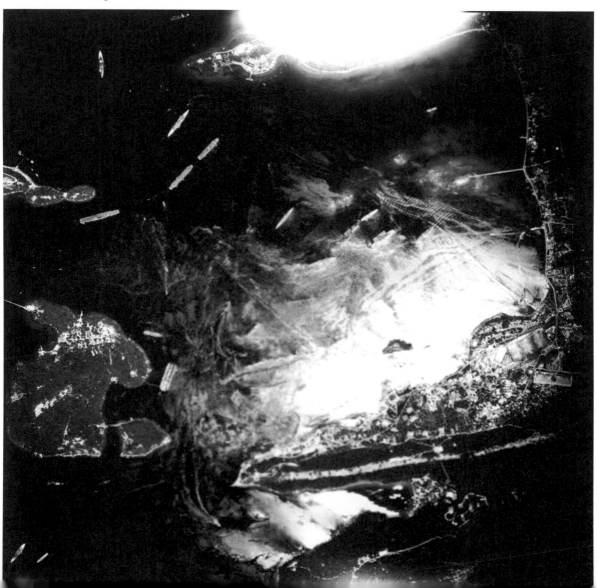

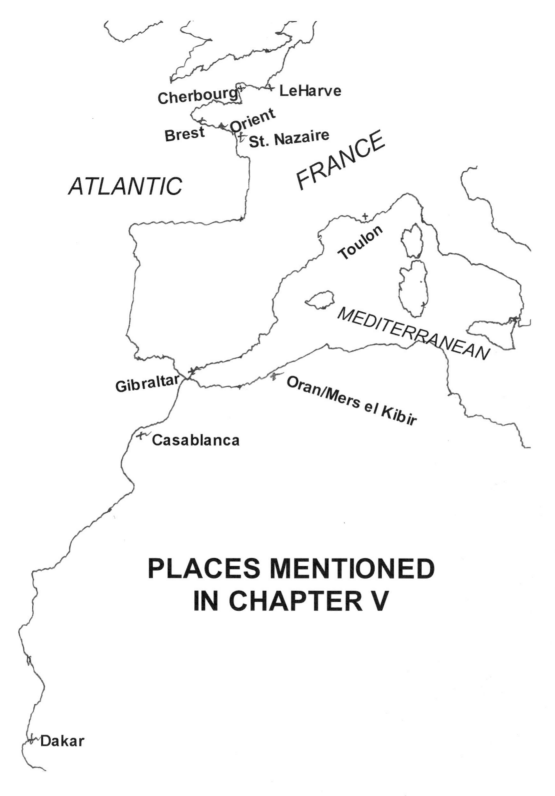

PLACES MENTIONED
IN CHAPTER V

CHAPTER VI
IMPERIAL JAPANESE NAVY

With the 1931 publication of Herbert O. Yardley's book The American Black Chamber, Japan learned the U.S. was reading coded diplomatic instructions during the Washington Naval Treaty negotiations in 1921-22 and pushed the Japanese negotiators down to secret Tokyo-set bottom limits in every ship category. The Imperial Japanese Navy (IJN) was recognized as the world's third largest navy, but resentment was high as they felt the Western Powers had tricked them and didn't consider them an equal. The Japanese were further insulted when the League of Nations wanted to meddle in affairs in China, which Japan considered in their Sphere of Influence, causing Japan to walk out of the League in 1933.

They began to ignore the Naval Treaty limits and, in 1936, did not participate in the Second London Naval Treaty discussions. Japan began pushing south and west into China from Manchuria which they'd occupied earlier in the decade. They were also expanding their empire east by fortifying islands in the Marshall and Caroline Islands (given them for siding with the victors in World War I). All that took more guns, tanks, ships and planes. The Pacific Arms Race was on.

The IJN air arm was tested in China and performed well but had no opposition to speak of. The same was true of ships up to light cruiser size. Larger warships had no opportunity to test their mettle.

Ever xenophobic, the island nation with distinct people and language, and a highly developed police system down to individual neighborhoods, was easily closed down to outsiders. Always difficult, by the middle 1930s it was nearly impossible for Western agents and Attachés to get close enough to pick up details of IJN fleets or units under construction. Western spies and sources in Japan were almost non-existent.[1] Unlike in Europe, there were no U.S. or British bases, and no aircraft with the range, to overfly IJN fleet bases, so the West had no aerial photo cover of Japanese shipyards or naval anchorages. Few people in Western Intelligence organizations spoke Japanese. Japanese Naval codes were still largely a mystery. Radio ranges to Japanese anchorages were long, making for shallow angles of intercept from any one station, limiting precise RDF locational accuracy, though the U.S. Navy strove to compensate by catching signals in Hawaii; Midway Island; Guam; Sitka and Dutch Harbor, Alaska; Bainbridge Island, Washington; San Diego, Eureka and Point Arguello, California; American Samoa and Oahu, Territory of Hawaii (also Corregidor in the Philippines until it fell early in the war). Some of those stations also captured IJN message traffic and forwarded it for decoding.

During advances to Hawaii and as far west as Ceylon (also later to the Coral Sea and Midway) the IJN quickly proved they could maintain exceptional radio discipline and deception. The net result was that Allied Intelligence didn't know much about the Japanese Navy except when it was on the offensive and didn't see IJN ships except when they were under attack by Allied air or submarine.[2] Since many of the IJN ships so attacked after mid-1942 wound up sunk, photos of them were more historic than helpful to Allied Intelligence.

Unlike other Axis belligerents, Japan presented a major surface threat, entering WW II with ten carriers, eleven battleships, eighteen heavy and twenty light cruisers. Many of those were extensively rebuilt WW I hulls, but new ships building or working up in each class were among the best in the world. And the IJN's 24" torpedo was the best in the war.

176

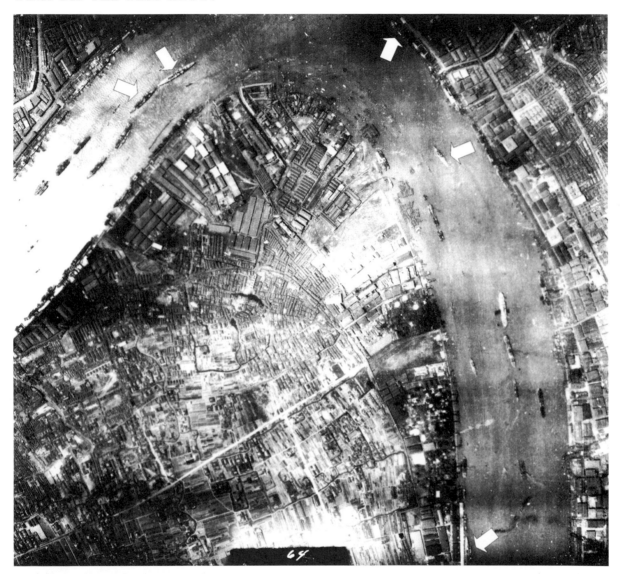

The short answer is, not much. There were "windows" onto the IJN, mostly where and when their ships went to foreign ports, such as Shanghai where their warships (but none of the big modern ships) often berthed near USN and Royal Navy vessels. A Japanese aircraft photographed Shanghai on 19 March 1935—of course we didn't see this until after the war. Two cruisers are anchored bow-to-stern midstream in the Huangpo at upper left, near the Bund (the business district just off the top of the photo). I scale the larger of the two at about 645 feet long. It appears to have two turrets forward and one aft, but I believe that's because lower aft turret is under canvas. She also appears to have an aircraft midships starboard side. Those two vessels are probably "westerners" (U.S. or British). An old warship, possibly IJN *Izumo*, is against the quay (top) and another midstream around the bend, also probably Japanese. Closer to the Yangtze is the unmistakable length-width ratio of a large CA (lower right arrow).

(Above) An old armored cruiser anchored opposite the Bund in 1937-38 is probably *Izumo*, the Japanese flagship during the "China Incident" that began on 7 July 37. A USN Attaché or sailor likely took the picture, but seeing the 1900 vintage warship close up didn't add anything to our understanding of modern Japanese vessels.

Equally unhelpful was the photo (below) from Osaka in 1934. I can't tell if it was from an Attaché or a newspaper/magazine but something is wrong. Apparently it was taken with the sun low to the right, but the lights and darks don't work quite right. Perhaps it has been copied too many times, picking up contrast with each generation—but there is the Japanese navy. There are five battleships (nearest the camera) and perhaps six cruisers. Raw numbers is all anyone was going to get from this picture, illustrating the paucity of information and sources on pre-war IJN. Still, anything and everything the Japanese would let out was dutifully clipped or copied and forwarded to Headquarters.

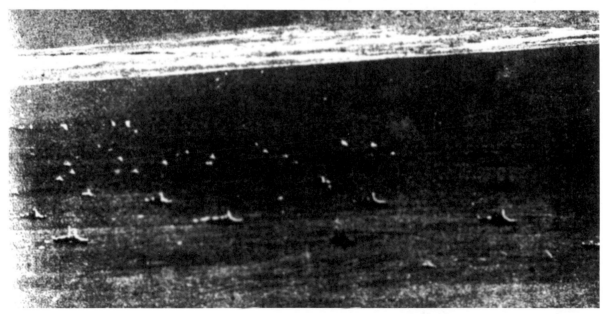

More typical and more helpful is this photo of CV *Hosho*, Japan's first "purpose built" carrier. Made with British help and loosely following contemporary Royal Navy design, she was commissioned in 1922. Her island and mast were removed in 1923 and the flight deck was extended to the bow in the late 1930s, helping date this photo. Note originally folding funnels (each a slightly different size) were now fixed upright.

Hosho was designed to carry twenty six aircraft but as planes became larger and heavier that number shrank to fifteen during the "China Incident" and eight or nine for WW II (she was unable to handle the most modern aircraft—Zero, Val and Kate).

She was too slow to "run with the big boys" and, after providing fleet support during the Midway Battle, was relegated to training in the Inland Sea, allowing her to survive the war.

Also typical of pre-war Intelligence collection is this photo of Light Cruiser *Jintsu*. An ONI note on the neg. said "may be retouched." Photos such as this were useful for ship recognition but little else. This CL participated in the "China Incident", invasion of the Philippines, the Java Sea battles, was command ship for destroyers that gave the Allies fits in the Solomon Islands, and was sunk on 13 July 1943 during surface action in the Battle of Kolombangara. The numbers in both lower corners are file locations for retrieval of the negative.

The photo below is where ship recognition really comes into play. Amanohashidate on Miyazu Bay near Kyoto. The narrow tree-lined causeway at the bottom is the "Bridge to Heaven" that is traditionally to be viewed by bending over and looking between your legs. One of our "tourist" Attachés in the late 30s caught CV *Hosho*, with two *Nagara*-class light cruisers (three stacks), two *Naka*-class light cruisers (four stacks), and 12 DD (*Momi*-class nearest the camera and *Kamikaze*-class in the background).

The Attaché photo (above) was easy to ID—three *Mutsuki*-class Destroyers moored off the Shanghai Bund in 1938-39. Twelve of these 37 knot DDs were built. Almost light cruisers in capability, they carried four 4.7" guns, ten torpedoes, more than a dozen each depth charges and mines and numerous machine guns. None of them survived the war.

Below is a more interesting photo, though difficult to date. From top to bottom, a light cruiser of *Naka*-class and four battleships. The top two BB are *Ise* and *Hyuga* after some mid-1930s rebuilding of their pagoda masts. Note the six twin-turrets mounting 14" naval rifles. In 1943, as a stop-gap for carrier losses at Midway, these two BB had flight decks installed extending from the last turret amidships to the stern. The so-called hermaphrodite battleships never contributed much to the war with either guns or aircraft.

Second ship from the bottom is a *Kongo*-class BB, probably *Kirishima* (identified by the distance between the two aft turrets and the larger, taller fore-funnel). Based upon the forward funnel trunked aft, the BB nearest the camera is probably *Mutsu*. Configuration of these four ships suggests a date for the photograph around 1931 or a little earlier (*Mutsu* got a "clipper bow" in 1930 and sistership *Nagato* didn't get hers until 1936).

Battleships lined up like this suggests an IJN publicity photo picked out of a magazine by one of our operatives, but I'm sure ONI was glad to get it.

180

It was rare for an Attaché to get close enough to photograph a ship in building. This BB hull matches *Ise*, launched in 1915, and probably dates from her extensive reconstruction at Kure in 1934-37.

(Right) The forward funnel trunked aft makes this 16"-gun BB *Mutsu* in a publicity photo. The bow is too indistinct for positive ID or date but I'd guess it is in the early 1930s.

Below is the same battleship class. I've left the file caption on to demonstrate that "Military Intelligence" before WW II was essentially a librarial function. The photo clearly came from an "open source" and those filing it not only couldn't read Japanese but didn't know much about the IJN ships. The BB is most likely *Mutsu* between 1924 and 1930.

JAP NAVY -- battleship without English identification, but see Japanese characters in lower corners. (Nagato?)

Wide spacing between the two aft main 14"-gun turrets was distinctive to BB *Haruna*, *Hiei*, *Kongo* and *Kirishima*. *Kongo*, launched in 1913, was the last IJN battleship built outside Japan (Vickers & Sons in the UK). Her sisters used the same plan but were built at Yokosuka, Nagasaki and Kobe, Japan, between 1911 and 1915. All were "modernized" in the late 1920s and early 30s to provide, among other things, lengthening aft, more deck armor, better torpedo protection and the towering "pagoda fore-mast" that became a key recognition feature for all IJN battleships. Each "pagoda" was slightly different. This is probably *Kirishima* in the late 30s. Sailors on deck seem to be work parties not "manning the side" for a ceremony.

Japanese heavy cruisers were ranked among the best in the world. *Atago* carried ten 8" guns in five turrets and had speed above 35 knots (pretty much the norm for an IJN CA and several knots faster than U.S. heavy cruisers). She and sister ships *Takao*, *Maya* and *Chokai* also carried the marvelous oxygen-driven "Long-Lance" 24-inch torpedo. The high sloping flat front face of the superstructure was a key recognition feature for this class.

Below, Heavy Cruiser *Nachi* was in a class with *Ashigara*, *Haguro* and *Myoko*, all built between 1924 and 1929 (a few years earlier than *Takao*-class so their superstructures were a little less elaborate). In this photo the cruiser still has side turrets with single 4.7" guns—they were replaced with twin 5" guns in the mid-30s. Western nations had a good look at this class when *Ashigara* visited England and Germany in 1937. All ships of this class were modernized again just before the war.

A more significant photo was of CV *Soryu* with the top of her island just showing, possibly during sea trials not long after her commissioning in 1937 (riding high and no planes evident). She took part in the Pearl Harbor attack and was sunk at Midway. Extreme enlargement shows this photo was a high quality half-tone, so a USN Attaché probably clipped it out of a magazine, again emphasizing that America didn't know much about intelligence or intelligence gathering before WW II.

183

Probably no more enlightening, but interesting, the following two photos were certainly taken before the war but didn't come into the hands of U.S. Intelligence until they were found on Kiska in 1943 after invading Japanese were gone.

At left, a single gun firing from a BB, possibly ranging during an exercise. Built-up structure around the funnel and two turrets immediately aft suggests BB *Hyuga* is in the background.

We might have profited from seeing the photo below before the war. It is the launch of a Type 93 24-inch diameter "Long-Lance," the torpedo with three times the range of what the USN was using—and IJN ships could reload and fire again where U.S. shipboard torpedoes were a one-shot deal. This weapon did terrible damage to our ships in South Pacific surface engagements early in the war when our own torpedoes were often failing.

These typical photos from the pre-war files make it obvious that the Japanese were willing to let the west see things they couldn't hide, like ships in port, but skillfully fended foreign eyes (and ears) off of anything of importance.

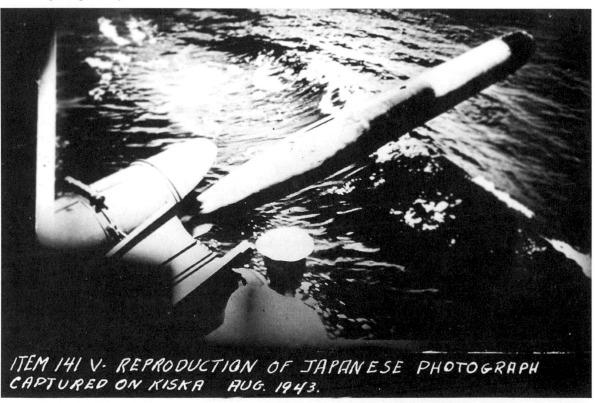

ITEM 141 V. REPRODUCTION OF JAPANESE PHOTOGRAPH CAPTURED ON KISKA AUG. 1943.

184

PEARL HARBOR

In April 1940 the U.S. Pacific Fleet left its anchorage at San Pedro, California for an annual "Fleet Problem" half way across the Pacific at Pearl Harbor, Territory of Hawaii. In May, President Roosevelt directed the ships to remain in Hawaii. His decision supported China by potentially threatening Japanese supply lines to oil in Indonesia and Japanese efforts to interdict western supplies to Nationalist China, but it also made his own fleet vulnerable. The Japanese would never have dreamed of an attack on the West Coast of the United States but Hawaii was well within their reach—and within the realm of possibility.

Several USN war games in the 1930s featured carrier attacks on Pearl Harbor using dive bombers. The Royal Navy added torpedoes to the tactics by their successful November 1940 attack on Italian capital ships at Taranto. Japanese planners studied USN Hawaiian exercises and the Taranto attack and shaped an attack of their own that improved on every aspect. Most important, they rigged their excellent 17.7" aerial torpedoes with wooden fins to let them run in the shallow waters of Pearl Harbor, using Southeast Loch to get the needed distance. They added fins to 16" naval rifle armor-piercing projectiles to be delivered by dive bombing.

Surprise was achieved and the attack came close to crippling U.S. naval capability in the Pacific. Four battleships were damaged, four sunk, leaving the USN with six operational BB weeks away in the Atlantic.[3] The IJN hoped to draw what was left of the U.S. Pacific Fleet into a surface gun battle that they would easily win. They also intended that the Pearl Harbor attack would sink or damage at least two of the three U.S. Pacific Fleet aircraft carriers.[4] *Enterprise* and *Lexington* had been in Pearl a few days earlier but both were at sea to the west on the morning of 7 December 1941.

American Intelligence files and National Archives contained photos of the Pearl Harbor attack from the ground (the U.S. side) but none from the IJN side were unearthed until after the war, and not all of those are actually from the 7 December attack.

Even following Japanese successes in Hawaii, at Wake Island, Guam, in the Dutch East Indies and the Philippines, the U.S. still didn't know much about IJN Order of Battle, ship capabilities, ship locations or operational intentions. The Allies still couldn't overfly major IJN anchorages for imagery so RDF, SIGINT, submarine reports and chance sightings were the only windows onto the locations, status and operations of this formidable foe.

As Admiral Yamamoto predicted, for about six months the IJN raged across the Pacific at will, pushing into the Solomon's, New Guinea, Indonesia and even to the waters off Ceylon (with their forces being spread thinner and thinner). For the next five months neither side had clear dominance in the push-and-shove. Then the tide began to turn and, despite occasional localized successes after the fall of 1942, never turned back again.

IJN warships weren't met directly until the Coral Sea Battle in early May of 1942, and then it was carrier vs. carrier. The same battle was fought a month later off Midway Island, and the IJN disaster was so stunning that knowledge of the loss was suppressed in Japan.

USN and IJN surface ships met in the Solomon's and this time the American government had to suppress public knowledge of the disastrous results. A series of sharp surface engagements, showed the effectiveness of IJN cruisers and destroyers, but they were being used in support of lines of communication and ground forces. When USN carriers were involved the battles were either inconclusive or losses for the Japanese.

Heavy American, Australian and British warships relocated from the Atlantic, were replacing Allied losses and western industry was beginning to roll out new ships.

Japanese failure to destroy heavy marine repair facilities and fuel oil tank farms in Hawaii proved a major mistake as Pearl Harbor recovered quickly and became a jumping-off place for USN ships, particularly submarines. The net result of the Pearl Harbor attack forced the U.S. to drop the battleship vs. carrier debate and shift to an offense strategy centered on carrier aircraft and submarines, a pattern of combat the IJN couldn't sustain and producing losses they couldn't replace.

I.D. 3657

EARLY WAR YEARS

Once hostilities began the only way the Allies got a look at IJN resources was in combat and our airmen and sailors were usually far too busy to take pictures. The lack of even rudimentary photoreconnaissance over ports used by the Japanese (Singapore, Brunei, Cam Ranh Bay, Rabaul, Truk and others) was a distinct disadvantage for the Allies but Japanese aerial recon was equally blind (in part because it was so primitive technically).

A rare look at Yokosuka Naval Base on Tokyo was provided by the Doolittle Raiders on 18 April 1942. Just above the B-25 nacelle is probably the old (1900) Armored Cruiser *Azuma*. At lower left is 1905 Armored Cruiser *Kasuga*. Neither played a role in the war and, as will be seen later, both were in these same locations in 1945. A photo taken by the raiders seconds earlier was out the left cockpit window so they were apparently using a hand-held personal camera. A few seconds later their flight track took them almost directly over the graving dock where the giant carrier *Shinano* was building in secret, but the Doolittle flyers weren't briefed to collect Intelligence and apparently didn't see it or didn't know to photograph it.

Naval actions in the Dutch East Indies, the Philippines and Indian Ocean yielded no Intelligence, only Allied losses. The next look the west got at major IJN warships was during a carrier-to-carrier battle in the Coral Sea, the first of its kind and an engagement neither side expected. That battle was a draw—the first time that the IJN didn't prevail in an offensive move. They lost a carrier and had another damaged and it rattled them—it also reduced the IJN carrier force that might have been in the Midway Battle.

The Doolittle Raid and rebuff in the Coral Sea resulted in an attempt to acquire a base in mid-Pacific as an outpost against American advances. Like the invasion of Wake Island, the IJN battle plan for taking Midway Island was overly complex, involving several fleets converging and a thrust at Alaska to draw the USN north. Unfortunately for them, the USN had finally broken into IJN codes and knew what to expect. The Midway photos below all came from Army bombers attacking before the crucial naval engagement. Land-based bombers from Midway Island attacked the Japanese ships on 4 June 1942, causing them to break-course, but it was quickly apparent that one of the safest places to be in WW II was on a fast-moving warship attacked by high-flying horizontal bombers.

186

I've seen this photo identified as several different carriers at Midway. In fact it is *Shoho* during Coral Sea. The intent of the "camouflage" is obscure. This photo must be from early in the battle. There is debris and evidence of bomb damage (as well as people effecting repairs) on the deck. She went down on 7 May 1942 south of Woodlark Island.

(Below) One of the Midway carriers at speed, probably *Kaga*, 4 June 1942.

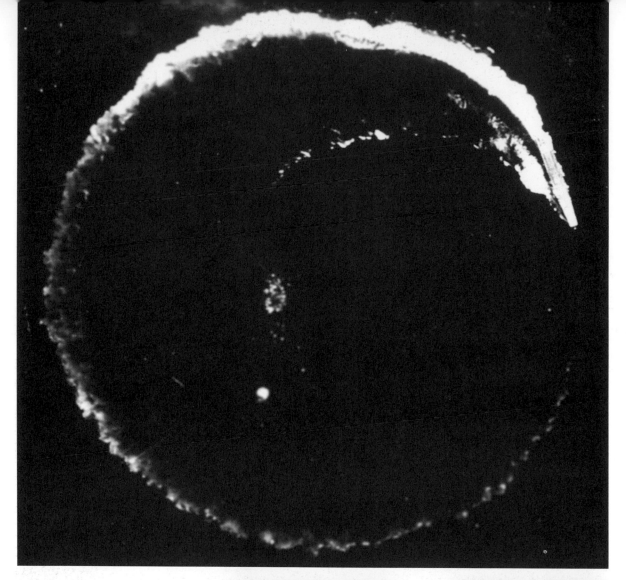

(Above) *Soryu* easily evading bombs, 4 June 1942.

Enlargement of *Soryu* early in the Midway battle. Wingspan shadow measured against the carrier's 69' beam suggests the aircraft spotted for take-off is a Mitsubishi A6M2 "Zero" but the shape of the wing doesn't seem quite right for a positive ID.

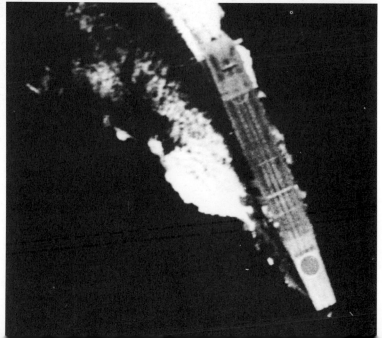

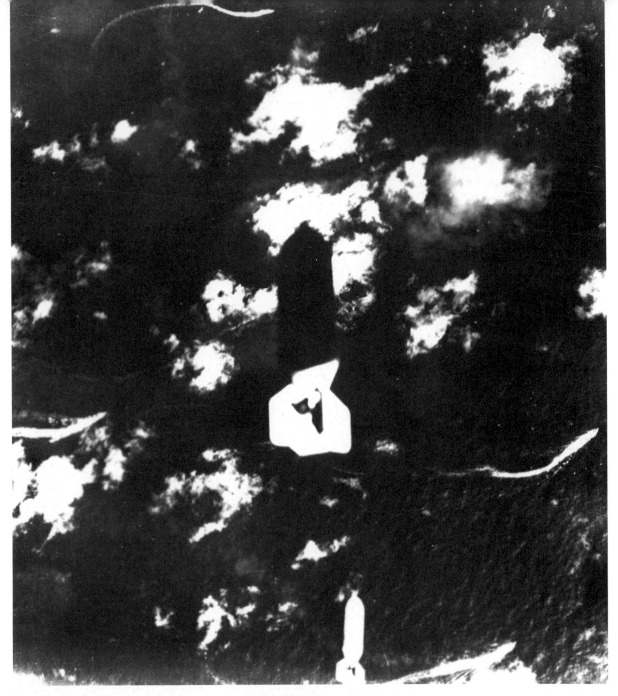

Above, flying from 25,000 feet, B-17s from Midway tried to hit Japanese ships on 4 June. The time is given as 1355 hrs. The fact that no enemy fighters intervened suggests this was bombing of the "Invasion Force" which had no carriers attached. Image quality precludes ship identification but my sense is that two battleships are at bottom right, a heavy cruiser is at the left and a cruiser and destroyer are at the top (based mainly upon length-to-width ratios). No hits were recorded. High altitude horizontal bombing of fast maneuvering ships was generally a waste of time and effort—but might unnerve a captain.

189

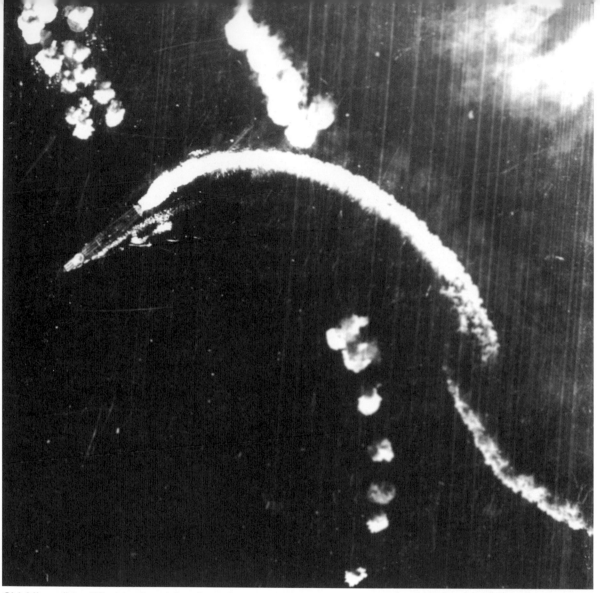

CV *Hiryu* (identified by her island on the port side) on 4 June, easily evading a strike by horizontal bombers at 20,000'. Enlargement shows two "Zero" fighters on alert near the island, their characteristic swept back leading wing edge shows clearly (possibly a third in the island's shadow). A contemporary caption claimed this was *Akagi* "hit by 431st Bomb Sq," a unit normally based in Hawaii, flying out of Midway Island. Actually, there were no hits and the B-17 was fortunate the "Zero's" didn't come up to say hello.

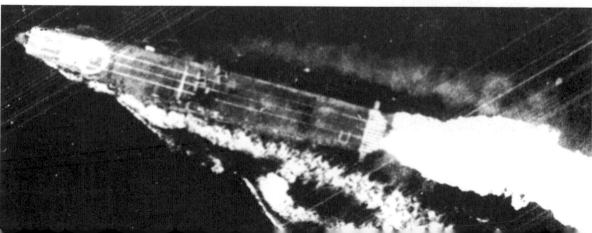

The IJN savaged USN surface vessels in the Solomon Islands and around New Guinea, boldly sending battleships to shell Henderson Field, but building Allied air and ground strength held and by September the tide was turning. (Above) DD *Yayoi* was sunk by British and American planes near Vakuta Island north of Papua, New Guinea.

I ran across few photos of IJN submarines in retired Intelligence Files, but they had some very large, long-ranging versions. Several made the trip to Europe to exchange technology with the Nazis. These pictures are from *I-34* visiting Brest on 3 October 43.

This ship was tracked by ULTRA. On 13 November 1943, during its voyage back to Japan, *I-34* was sunk by a British sub off Panay, Malaysia—the first IJN submarine sunk by a Royal Navy sub.

Most Japanese subs were sunk by Allied submarines or destroyers.

191

I-34 welcomed by German sailors and officials on her 3 October 1943 arrival at Brest. These photos must have come into our hands via a "neutral observer."

Proof that ULTRA let Royal Navy Intelligence know about the Japanese visit, an RAF photo recce plane timed its overflight of Brest to catch the IJN submarine just off the harbor.

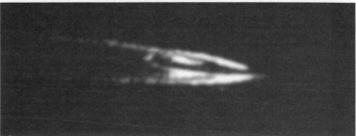

193

Reaching out from the Solomon's and New Guinea, the Allies were soon attacking, a variety of Japanese ships. This is a freighter converted to a seaplane tender. It had thirteen single-float bi-planes on deck when seen off New Britain Island on 11 October 1942. Note circular "gun tubs" fore and aft. Straight-wing planes are Nakajima E8N "Dave," elliptical wings are probably Mitsubishi F1M "Pete," both ideal for use in the airfield sparse islands.

The water splash at far right indicates an attack, but post-war records show none of the nine similar vessels hit or sunk this day.

(Below) A USN *Curtiss* SOC scout from a cruiser, photographed a pair of IJN battleships being attacked on 26 October 1943 (the small bomb-splash is more harassment than attack). The critical Battle of Santa Cruz Island was also going on 400 miles east, but I think this photo is in the Solomon's.

I suspect these are BBs *Haruna* and *Kongo* in the waters north of Guadalcanal. They had been shelling Henderson Field with some regularity. Five sea battles were fought in these waters between 4 August and 30 November (Savo Island, Cape Esperance, First and Second Guadalcanal, and Tassafaronga).

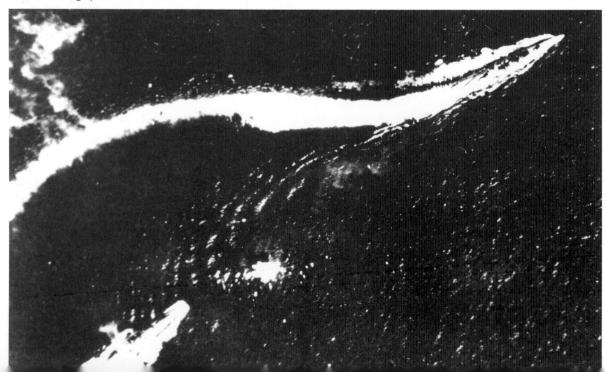

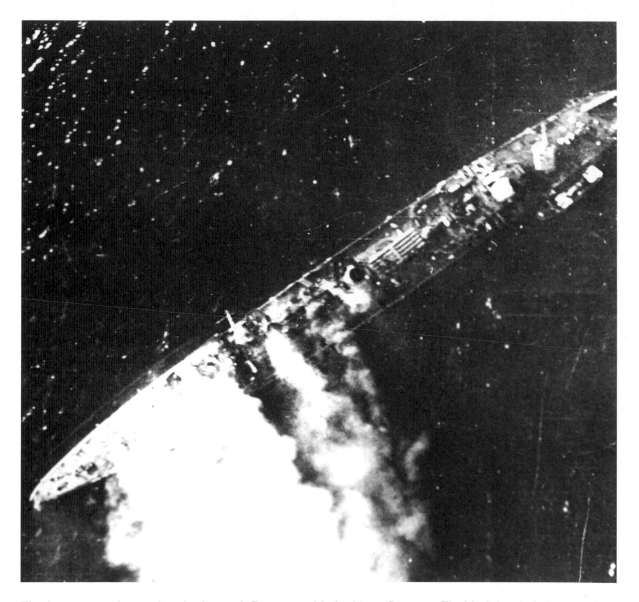

The hunter was becoming the hunted. Destroyer *Yudachi*, on fire near Florida Island, Solomon's, 13 November 1942. She was damaged by gunfire in the First Naval Battle of Guadalcanal during which an IJN force of two BB, a cruiser and eleven DDs attempted to shell Henderson Field (Guadalcanal's airfield) and land reinforcements. Five USN cruisers and eight DDs tried to block. In a ferocious, unusually close-range night battle (at which the IJN excelled), involving torpedoes and searchlights as well as gunfire, all but one of the USN cruisers and one DD were sunk or seriously damaged. Among the lost was USN Light Cruiser *Juneau* (CL-52) which went down with the five Sullivan brothers. The IJN lost two destroyers (one of them above) and over the next two days aircraft from Henderson Field sank the damaged Battleship *Hiei* and 11 transports with troops and supplies intended for Japanese forces on Guadalcanal.

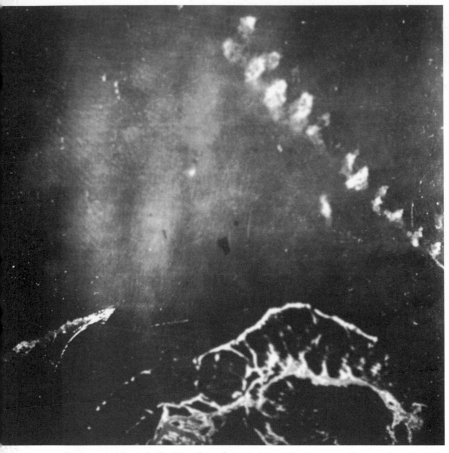

(Left) The day following the initial night engagement, a USN scout plane photographed what is beyond doubt a battleship retiring from the battle. I believe this is *Kirishima* because she is making good speed and trailing no oil. Damaged sister-BB *Hiei* would have had destroyers near-by to assist—and was in the process of being sunk by planes from USS *Enterprise*. This battleship appears to be alone, but there is a distinct smoke trail or wake just disappearing off the right side of the photo. Those "puffs" diagonalling across the photo are probably bomb impacts in the water going after the ship we don't see. If so, they represent the "stick" bomb-load of a large horizontal bomber, not the more random dispersal of individual bomb drops from carrier planes.

Kirishima was caught and sunk on 15 November west of Savo Island, by close-in fire from two USN battleships, during the Second Naval Battle for Guadalcanal. It was those battles that gave Sealark Channel its more familiar name of "Iron Bottom Sound."

(Below) A contemporary caption says this is USS *Cushing* on 13 November 1942, but we know that DD was listing heavily at dawn and sank at 1700 hrs. The sun is well up and this ship shows no list. It's hard to see detail necessary for an ID but this looks like it could be IJN DD *Murasame*, photographed by the same aircraft as above, "between Guadalcanal and Florida Island." *Murasame* was damaged during the night surface naval battle near Savo Island, but not sunk.

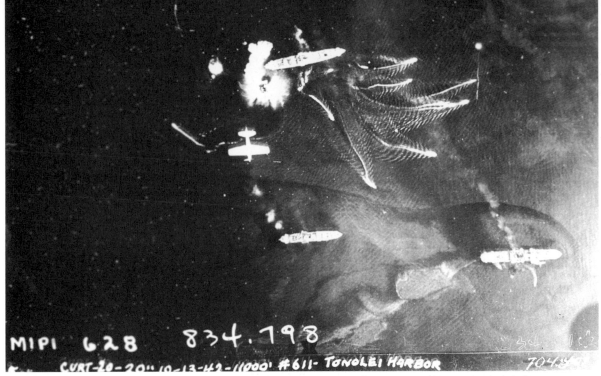

MIPI 628 834.798

CURT-20-20" 10-13-42-11000' #611- TONOLEI HARBOR 704.

Aircraft flying from Henderson Field on Guadalcanal were a thorn in the side of every IJN unit within reach. (Above) Lighters are scattering as bombs drop in Tonolei Harbor, Bougainville. Both freighter/transport are identified as military by the paired round gun-tubs fore and aft. Note the open hatch on the upper vessel. The plane overhead is a "Cactus Airforce" Grumman F4F "Wildcat." The taking aircraft was at 11,000' altitude.

(Below) Heavy bombers based on New Guinea were also ranging wide to seek out IJN ships. This is off Amboina, Indonesia, supposedly bombing of an unidentifiable cruiser (at top left) on 21 January 1943. Actually the tanker at center right was a more important target as Japan was desperate to maintain a flow of oil to the homeland.

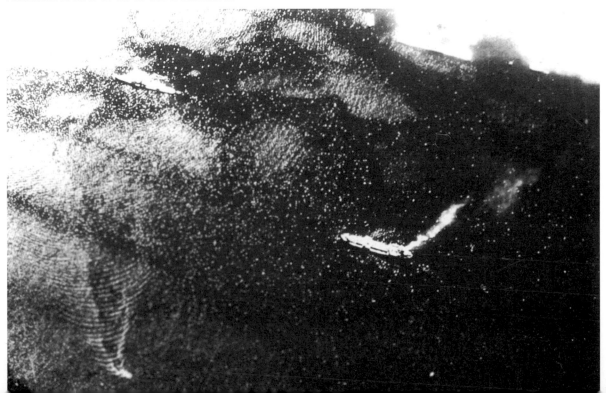

Despite increasing air opposition, IJN warships did not retreat to distant ports. Particularly from light cruiser down to destroyer escort and patrol boat, they were too important for keeping open supply lines to far-flung occupation detachments.

Of course that kept them vulnerable. Here what may be a *Fubuki*-class destroyer evaded bombs in March 1943. The tail skid showing in the photo identifies this attacker as a B-25.

Another IJN destroyer dodges a couple of bombs off Bougainville Island, 27 May 1943, possibly a *Kagero*-class.

Finchaven, New Guinea (60 miles east of Lae), 3 March 1943. Crewmen are clearly visible in this low pass by a U.S. A-20 over *Fubuki*-class DD *Shirayuki* (Thanks to Kevin Denlay and World Naval Ship Forum for help with the ID). The rails on deck are to move torpedoes for reloading.

Ever increasing Allied air activity resulted in diminishing Japanese fighter cover and allowed Allied medium bombers to range at will over Japanese lines of communication at sea, attacking everything they found. It also resulted in one of my favorite WW II photos.

Above left a B-25 of 499BS, 345BG bombing an enemy "ship" at Cape Wom (west of Wewak, Papua New Guinea), 22 March 1943.

More attacks meant more Japanese losses. (Above Right) A USN tug is salvaging an IJN submarine in the Solomon's, 21 April 1943.

(Left) Probably DD Nagatsuki, used to move troops to Guadalcanal, beached and burning after gunfire from USN cruisers and destroyers, near Kolombangara, New Georgia, 6 July 1943.

200

(Above photos) Research suggests this is DD *Mikazuki*, "wrecked off Cape Gloucester, 27 July 1943" and sunk by B-25s "the next day." These photos were clearly from a B-25. There is no wake showing the ship underway, and she looks down at the bow but the date is given as 29 July.

(Right and below) Two photos of a freighter and sub-chaser under attack near Wewak on 2 September 1943. In the lower enlargement two B-25s are at upper left and you can see bomb separation from the upper plane. This is a low altitude attack, but is using normal bombing techniques.

"Skip bombing" was a more successful technique. The attacker came in close and very low, skipping its bombs over the water into a target hull (reminiscent of the Mohne Dam raid only using standard bombs), increasing the probability of a hit. This 18 October 1943 attack was at Vunapope, New Britain Island (southeast of Rabaul); the target a Patrol Boat.

The photo below is another of my all-time favorites. It shows a perfectly executed skip-bomb attack on a Japanese ship, 11 June 1943. I can't see enough to ID the ship type but perhaps the most interesting thing about this encounter is that the 400BS was flying B-24s out of Port Moresby, New Guinea—a plane a bit large, ungainly to be attacking ships at 200 feet, leading me to suspect the target was something lightly armed, or a merchant vessel.

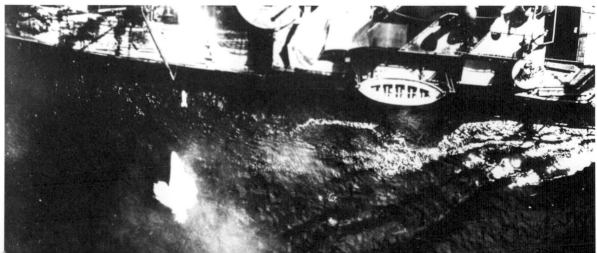

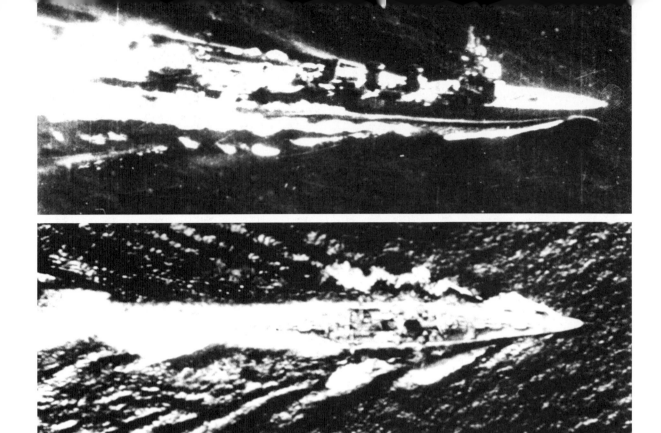

(Far Top) Skip bombing worked well against freighters and light warships but, because of the requirement to be "on the deck" and overfly the target, was seldom tried against ships with more anti-aircraft guns—particularly when the target was maneuvering at speed. Mushroom funnel-caps identify this as the Light Cruiser *Kuma*. She was photographed 100 miles north of Papua, New Guinea on 28 October 1943.

(Above) A *Mogami*-class heavy cruiser (the stack suggests *Suzuya*) at speed about 250 miles north of New Ireland on 9 October 1943. Note three float-planes just forward of the two aft turrets.

(Left) A *Kagero*-class destroyer appearing dead in the water. The date is hard to read, and made more difficult because in those years some U.S. units titled film month-day-year. My guess for this photo is 4 May 1943.

618053

A SHRINKING EMPIRE

The IJN had far-flung outposts in the Gilbert, Marshall and Caroline Islands, but they were considered a "trip wire" for the Empire, functioning as unsinkable carriers, contributing no resources. They were supported from the large lagoon at Truk in the eastern Caroline Islands. Allied carrier action against those scattered enclaves didn't result in the head-on naval clashes seen in the Solomon's because the USN arrived suddenly and in force, then was gone, giving the IJN no chance to respond. Besides, other than Imperial Pride, there was no reason to go all out to save obviously expendable locations.

Such was not the case in the Solomon Islands. They were the door to New Guinea and that was the road to the Philippines and Netherlands East Indies—and the oil Japan needed so desperately.

Japanese naval strength dominating the Solomon's and Eastern New Guinea was based on Rabaul on the north end of New Britain Island which they occupied in January-February 1942. Nearly four hundred anti-aircraft guns defended Rabaul. Four airfields hosted twin-engine bombers that ranged to New Guinea and Guadalcanal, and some of the finest, most deadly, IJN Naval aviators in the Pacific (including multiple ace Saburo Sakai). The magnificent natural anchorage of Simpson Harbor sheltered IJN ships as well as the freighters, tankers and troopships vital to maintaining Japanese lodgments to the south. Those footholds were not expendable.

Initially, Allied Intelligence knew little about Rabaul beyond the pre-war photo above.

Steady Allied advances put Rabaul within reach of an increasing number of Allied land-based aircraft. The Solomon's air war became a slugging match between Rabaul's four airfields and the three airfields on "The Canal."

Left is the earliest vertical coverage of Rabaul I ran across. The date is given as 5.9.42. Based upon USAAF practices at that time, I believe it is 9 May 1942. If so, it was probably taken by a B-17 from Townsville, Australia. There are nine four-engine flying boats in the water (eight along the upper coast), two probable cruisers and over two dozen large ships, mostly freighters. The large light colored area at upper right is Vukanau Airfield being rapidly expanded by the Japanese. Those black puff shapes are just shadows from clouds.

The first task was getting a good look at Rabaul for making charts and target folders. Acquiring comprehensive aerial coverage was a high priority, but the range from U.S. bases was long and overflying several Wings of Zeros wasn't a walk in the park.[5]

Beginning in February 1942 American carrier planes had bombed the Japanese Rabaul bastion on New Britain Island, in an attempt to take pressure off the lower Solomon's and New Guinea.

In the first eleven days of November 1943 Rabaul was struck by Army and USN aircraft with the largest attack on 2 November. Fifth Air Force launched a major strike, using 75 medium bombers (B-25s) flying at low altitude, in an operation designed to disrupt Japanese capability to interfere with the Invasion of Bougainville Island.

Rabaul under attack, 2 November 1943. The photo above was taken out the tail of one of the B-25s, shows bombs going off and freighters burning. A *Takao*-class heavy cruiser (possibly *Atago*) working up speed in Simpson Harbor is identified by a raked fore-funnel and smaller perpendicular aft-funnel.

(Below) A B-25 of 90BS, 3BG races away from Simpson Harbor on 2 November. When USN carrier planes attacked three days later there were four heavy and one light cruiser here, all positioned to contest the anticipated Allied landings on Bougainville Island, 200 miles to the southeast.[6]

The 30 December 1942 photo (right) illustrates why Rabaul continued to be such an important target. Warships from Simpson Harbor attacked U.S. ships. Freighters from here were the life-line for Japanese troops in the Solomon's and New Guinea. The photo shows only part of the harbor, but there are 39 freighters, three DDE/Patrol boats, two large DD or light cruisers, two submarines and four Kawanishi H6K "Mavis" flying boats (two afloat, two on shore). Stippling near the center was probably caused by bottom disturbance from recent aerial bombing. If so, the clustered pattern indicates heavy bombers did the work.

The photo below was identified as an "Escort boat" by 400th Bomb Squadron personnel unsuccessfully attacking from 6000' in their B-24. It is north of Papua, New Guinea, 4 November 1943. This may be a *Yugumo*-class DD...definitely too fast and maneuverable for a horizontal bombing target.

206

New Hanover Island, 16 February 1944.

(Right) An enlargement of the previous photo shows crewmen on the sub-chaser abandoning their 40mm gun for shelter on the lee side of the superstructure as a pair of 499th Bomb Squadron B-25s from Dobodura Airfield, New Guinea, make skip-bomb passes. Other B-25s are attacking ships in the background. Off New Hanover Island, 16 February 1944.

The Japanese captain never altered course and it appears the bombs "skipped" right over his ship. Apparently the ships in the background weren't as lucky.

Ever since I found it in retired ONI files, I've considered this an interesting and unusual photo. The four-engine flying boat on deck is a Kawanishi H6K "Mavis" which gave me a scale (wingspan 131') and that led to ID of the ship (386' x 51'). She is the seaplane tender *Akitsushima*. The date is 30 March 1944, no location is given but it is likely in the Caroline Islands.

Japan still had plenty of commercial ships and warships on 5 November 1944 when a USN carrier aircraft took this photo of a "target rich environment" at Luzon. Note that some of the small destroyers and patrol craft are partially underwater, sinking or heavily damaged in earlier strikes. Desperation was beginning to set in. Keeping sea lanes open was critical to survival in the "home islands" but the size of the empire was shrinking and the enemy was clearly growing in strength.

Despite serious defeats into the fall of 1944, to its credit the IJN still did not retreat to the temporary safety of ports beyond the reach of Allied planes. The Japanese Navy was at sea and fighting to support deployed forces and keep sea lanes open.

OBLIQUE MOSAIC

JAPANESE TASK FORCE

FROM SORTIE CVL 29-37 OF 20 JUNE 1944

MIPI 25241 CONFIDENTIAL

1675, 313

ENCL. (A) TERPRON TWO REPORT NO. 38
INTERPRON TWO-43

(Above) A contemporary Intelligence graphic from the Battle of the Philippine Sea, also known as the "Great Marianas Turkey Shoot." It was the last carrier vs. carrier engagement of the war. Air combat at Midway and Guadalcanal had reduced the number of experienced IJN fighter pilots and two days of intense fighting on 19-20 June 1944 the U.S. Navy destroyed three IJN carriers and 600 aircraft, gutting Japanese Naval Aviation. Two photos were put together to show some of the IJN force assembled to oppose the U.S. invasion of Saipan in the Mariana Islands. I don't have the "gouge" so I don't know what the annotations mean. Scale/quality preclude much PI work, but wakes indicate speed and maneuverability of destroyers and cruisers. Annotation "3" is noticeably larger and shows no towering central superstructure, suggesting a carrier, probably Zuikaku (sister Shokaku was sunk the day before). Bomb splashes show concentration on that ship, and IJN carriers were always "target number one." Japan had nine carriers in the battle. Annotation "6" is a large ship, at least a heavy cruiser. Annotation "5" is too distant for much size comparison, but she has a flat, almost "carrier-like" profile.

(Above Left) DD attacked, 23 March 1943.

(Above right) Three IJN ships northeast of New Guinea, 3 March 1943. The one under attack is a probable cruiser.

THE LARGEST NAVAL BATTLE EVER FOUGHT

With Allied forces landing on Leyte to liberate the Philippines, the IJN came up with a typical Japanese plan involving forces converging from different directions and coordination they never seemed to achieve.[7] The aim was to get their heavy guns amid the soft transport off shore and inflict a devastating loss. To insure success, most of the remaining Japanese carriers, without planes, were dangled as bait to draw American carriers and fast battleships north away from the vulnerable transports. Surprise was essential, but unfortunately for the IJN, the Allies had submarines, surface ships and planes all over the area. The battle turned into a Naval Brawl of five or six separate actions that took three days to resolve and covered thousands of square miles of ocean. I found no aerial photos from the only battleship-to-battleship engagement (Surigao Strait, 24-25 October) and only one from Admiral Halsey's well-known chase after impotent Japanese carriers (Cape Engano, 25 October) that removed six U.S. battleships and thirteen cruisers from the crucial battle. The photos included here are from carrier aircraft trying to destroy the main IJN attack force. Fortunately planes from Halsey's seven carriers had the range to reach the most important combat from their "wild goose chase" launch positions northeast of Leyte

Early on 23 October USN submarines spotted the most formidable force, including BB *Yamato* and *Musashi*, coming north from Borneo. After radioing the alert, they sank Heavy Cruisers *Atago* and *Maya* and damaged CA *Takao*. Despite clear loss of surprise and firepower, the Japanese admiral (who was on CA *Atago* when she was sunk) raised his flag on *Yamato* and steamed on, knowing there would be a naval air attack the next day but counting on the "carrier bait" to the north drawing off many of the USN planes and confident in the raw naval power under his commanded. His fleet was now comprised of four battleships, seven heavy cruisers, two light cruisers and fifteen destroyers.

Battleships *Yamato* and *Musashi* were the centerpiece of the Japanese attack force. *Yamato* hadn't been seen at Midway but was in three or four encounters with USN submarines, including when *Skate* torpedoed her as she was returning to Truk in December 1943, but those were fleeting glimpses. Both BB were built masked by fences so western Attachés hadn't seen them before the war.[8] Both were battleship writ in large capital letters. At 71.6 K tons when their 862 foot hulls (*Musashi* was actually 23' shorter than her sister) worked up to 27 knots they were beyond amazing and into awesome. Three turrets mounting nine 18" naval rifles (the largest, most far-reaching guns mounted on a ship) gave them firepower to be reckoned with, and to top it off they were beautiful ships, the culmination of half a century of naval architecture and theoretically unsinkable. If the gods of war were fair, the IJN ultimate battleships would have had at least one chance to stand toe-to-toe with the best the U.S. Navy had, *South Dakota* or *Iowa*-class fast battleships,[9] but that was not to be. By late 1944 it was obvious that the age of heavy ship slug-fests was almost over (all but two IJN BB lost during the war went down to submarines and air attack. The second gun-action loss occurred on day two of the Leyte Gulf battle).

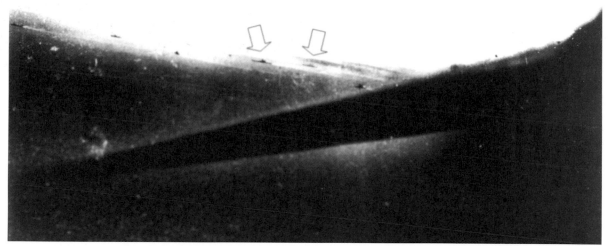

The first attacks on the main threat, the Center Force (sometimes called the Central Force), came at 0900 hours on 24 October 1944. The photo above is from an *Intrepid* (CV 11) aircraft, probably a Curtiss SB2C "Helldiver." It shows the two giant battleships near photo center and another BB showing just above the horizontal stabilizer. Location information on the photo indicates this is in the Tablas Straits, (western entrance to the Sibuyan Sea). The fact that two ships are "maneuvering" indicates some air attacks have already taken place but the main BB, with some 150 anti-aircraft guns each, are steaming ahead seemingly unperturbed.

I can just imagine the flurry of activity in the U.S. carrier force when this photo was developed and the Intel folks saw those two big fellows. The message their presence sent was unmistakable. Their superstructure appears like a right triangle with the base facing forward making *Yamato* and *Musashi* easy to track in the following photographs. They had long clean bows and distinctive, streamlined, silhouettes that were quite different from the towering "pagoda" superstructure masts of older IJN battleships. Compare with the two equally characteristic pyramidal superstructure appearance of the 159 feet shorter, USS *South Dakota*-class battleships below, photographed near Ponape on 1 May 1944.

211

A few minutes after the top photo an Intrepid aircraft caught the "pagoda-masted" BB *Nagato* just after a bomb dropped in her wake. Since she lost her cruiser escorts the day before, apparently CA *Myoko* or *Haguro* from the *Yamato* group had been attached to her.

(Below) Another *Intrepid* bomber caught *Nagato* and its consort closing on *Yamato* and *Musashi* (in all accounts, *Musashi* was positioned behind *Yamato*). Wake lengths indicate these ships have worked up to speeds above 20 knots (Nagato's top was 24kts). Clearly an air attack is underway.

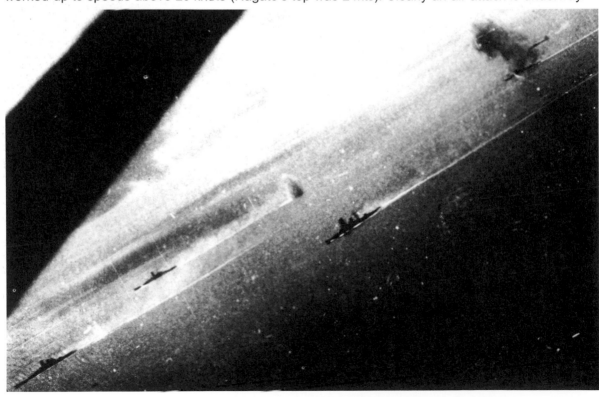

(Above) A second later a bomb hit on or near *Nagato*'s port bow. Flak and strafing splashes are showing all around *Musashi*. Strafing was used to suppress anti-aircraft fire.

(Below) *Intrepid* aircraft were still attacking. *Musashi* has reversed course and *Yamato* is out of the photo. *Nagato* is executing a flank-speed turn toward the departing bomber as a destroyer speeds between heavy cruisers on opposite courses.

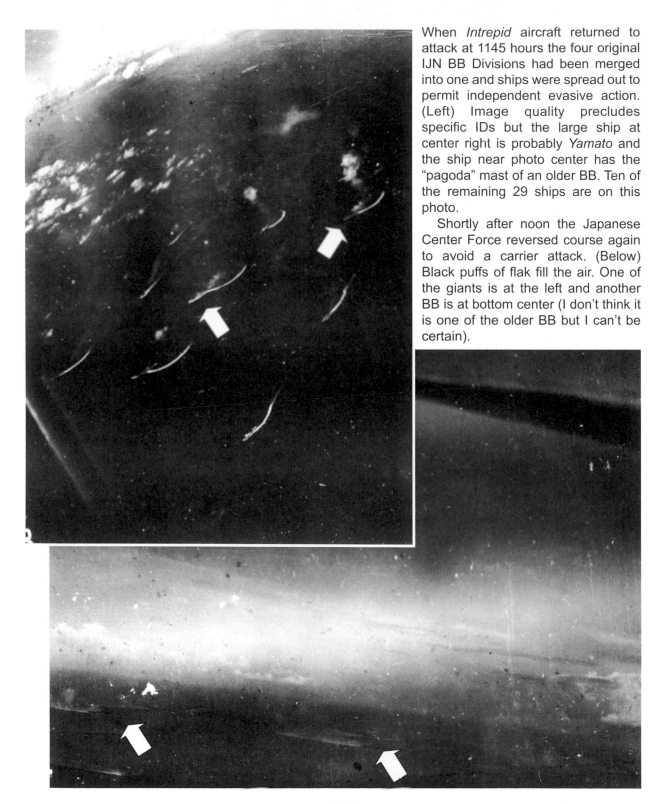

When *Intrepid* aircraft returned to attack at 1145 hours the four original IJN BB Divisions had been merged into one and ships were spread out to permit independent evasive action. (Left) Image quality precludes specific IDs but the large ship at center right is probably *Yamato* and the ship near photo center has the "pagoda" mast of an older BB. Ten of the remaining 29 ships are on this photo.

Shortly after noon the Japanese Center Force reversed course again to avoid a carrier attack. (Below) Black puffs of flak fill the air. One of the giants is at the left and another BB is at bottom center (I don't think it is one of the older BB but I can't be certain).

214

That's probably *Musashi* turning sharply and taking bomb hits on her starboard side. Wakes indicate seven ships on a parallel course going straight on. The largest wake (next one up) is probably from *Yamato* steaming ahead and to the right of her sister. The ship second from the top is one of the old BB and the ship nearest the left edge is probably the Light Cruiser *Yahagi*.

Another *Intrepid* bomber, likely part of the same bomb-run, took this photo at almost the same time and from a slightly different angle. CV 11 photo in Tablas Strait, 24 October 1944.

(Below) I can't tell which of the giants this is but it seems to have smoke coming off of something behind the stack—an area roughly equating to the hits sustained in the photo above. Beyond is probably the BB *Nagato*.

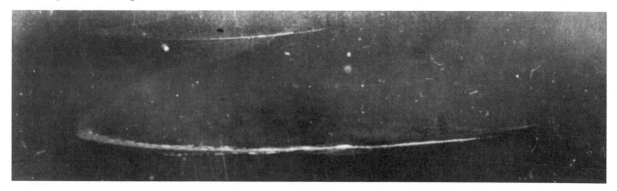

215

The caption for the photo above says this is *Musashi* taking hits in Tablas Strait but the mast and bow length don't look right to me. I believe it is actually *Nagato*.

By this time the Center Force had moved into the Sibuyan Sea and was less than a day's steaming from their objective—the vulnerable U.S. transports off Leyte.

During the early afternoon attacks, an aircrew flew directly over the IJN ships and got these images of *Yamato* and possibly *Kongo*.

(images are not to same scale)

By 1445 hours independent evasive maneuvers had scattered the Japanese ships.

At least six USN bombers are overhead (coming straight toward the camera) as the ships regroup. One of the older battleships is a faint shape with a long wake at photo center. Later in the afternoon, the fleet turned west to lengthen the range for USN carrier aircraft. Damaged *Musashi* went under and the ships turned back east. Believing the Center Force threat was over, Admiral Halsey charged north after the Northern Force and IJN aircraft carriers.

Carrier planes were back at 0945 hrs on the 25th and the flak was noticeably heavier. Individual ship IDs are impossible but *Yamato* is likely in the center of that smoke. The USN didn't yet know *Musashi* had sunk. The huge BB didn't go easy, finally succumbing to hits by twenty torpedoes and seventeen 1000 pound bombs plus another eighteen near-misses.

Up to this point, all the photographs I'd found were by three different aircraft from CV 11, USS *Intrepid*—though *Enterprise, Essex, Lexington, Franklin* and CVL *Cabot* were also involved. With no enemy air to worry about, back-seaters in some "Helldivers" and "Avengers" were documenting the battle using hand-held 6 3/8" focal-length Fairchild K-20 cameras that produced 4" x 5" exposures. On the morning of the 25th other carriers were doing the same thing. A 1000 hrs photo above from *Hancock* (CV 19) shows the unmistakable shape of Yamato (at left center) with old BB and heavy cruisers screening her. The Center Force was already disturbingly near the "soft" U.S. ships off Samar.

(Above) Another *Hancock* aircraft caught the "S" shaped wake of BB *Kongo* turning sharply to avoid what was probably a torpedo attack as the wake of a faster vessel streamed straight by. The plane taking the photo has apparently just passed over another ship in a hard turn; its wake is at lower right.

(Above) The same aircraft as above photographed a hit (or near miss) on what I identify as IJN BB *Kongo*. A heavy cruiser (upper left), also under attack, is on a nearly opposite course. Beyond the CA is a probable light cruiser.

(Below) Looking unscathed, *Yamato* at speed and under attack. Judging from wakes, apparently she didn't do much evading, relying on her AAA guns, speed and armor as she forged ahead for San Bernardino Strait and the "soft" targets off Samar.

220

This *Hancock* plane was so low over the water it must have been a torpedo-bomber. From right to left (page top to bottom) are *Yamato* and what looks like a possible destroyer in the blast at photo center. A heavy cruiser, probably *Haguro*, is taking several hits and/or near misses. The narrow, towering explosion and water column is typical of a torpedo hit (perhaps from the plane taking this picture). At far left (page bottom) is one of the older battleships, probably *Haruna*.

(this photo is shown as two pieces because my original was too large for me to capture in one scan)

Above, another *Hancock* torpedo plane, so low on the deck its prop is kicking up the water, got a good look at what is probably the Battleship *Kongo* in a hard turn to starboard.

A pair of Grumman TBF "Avenger" torpedo-bombers (at far left) from USS *Intrepid* zero in on a target while something at photo center is exploding. At least three other ships appear to be burning across the horizon at left.

(Below) TBFs from *Intrepid*, but probably not the same pair as above, pass an IJN vessel that seems fully afire. There is a lot of flak and at least two other ships appear to be burning. Another large ship, possibly one of the old BB is to the right of the sinking ship (straight below the ventral gun position on the TBF.

The Center Force broke out of San Bernardino Strait on 25 October and turned battleship guns on 18 milling USN escort carriers and 17 DD/DDE, in what has been called the Battle off Samar. With incredible élan U.S. destroyers and destroyer escorts charged battleships and cruisers, shielding the ungainly escort carriers with smoke and torpedo runs while aircraft from the CVEs, armed with high-explosive bombs intended for support to forces ashore, attacked as fast as they could sortie.

One U.S. CVE, two DD and one DDE were sunk off Samar and three CVE, one DD and two DDE damaged but it could have been a lot worse. The Japanese lost Heavy Cruisers *Chokai*, *Chikuma* and *Suzuya* and had *Haguro*, *Kumano* and *Tone* damaged. After two straight days of intense air attacks, unexpected resistance by USN destroyers, and the loss of many of his ships, Japanese Vice Admiral Kurita realized he couldn't achieve his objective, broke off the attack and retired the way he'd come.

Meanwhile, hundreds of miles north, Admiral Halsey's force of nine large and eight light carriers (with an aggregate of some 1100 planes), six fast battleships, four heavy cruisers, nine light cruisers and 57 destroyers ran down a Japanese force of one large and three light carriers (with a total of 108 planes), two BB, three CL and eight DD. In a massive USN air attack (the Japanese planes never saw the U.S. ships); all the IJN carriers were sunk along with a CL and two DD. One Japanese battleship and a light cruiser were damaged.

The only Intelligence file photo I came across from the Battle off Cape Engano was of a smoking, sinking *Zuikaku*, last of the Pearl Harbor attack carriers, on 25 October 1944.

The IJN Center Force sped west all night to get out of range but carrier planes found them early on the 26th. (Left) An "Avenger" from USS *Intrepid* photographed the Light Cruiser *Yahagi*, a frequent consort of *Yamato*. The CL is turning sharply and what is probably a DD (up and to the right) is making a similar turn to head in the opposite direction. Those strange black vertical shapes are tears in the original negative emulsion.

Five exposures later the same Intrepid "Avenger" spotted *Yamato* and what looks like *Nagato*

reversing course to evade bombs. Location is given as "Palawan Passage" so the Center Fleet was at the extreme range of USN carrier aircraft at this time.

Another seven exposures later caught one of the older battleships, possibly *Haruna*, crossing its own wake while another old BB comes up on the same new course (lower right). This neg. shows water spots from hasty processing.

Despite the extreme range, USN air attacks went on through the day.

(Below) A *Wasp* (CV 18) "Helldiver" photographed its wingmate after a low pass on a destroyer (that seems to be afire fore and aft). Time is 1500 hrs, location given as "South of Mindoro." Another warship can be seen reversing course in the background (up and right).

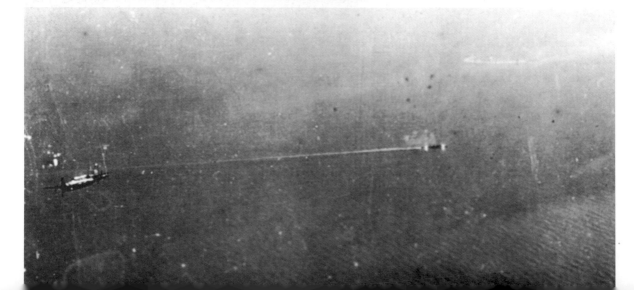

LEYTE GULF AFTERMATH

There were plenty of air attacks on Allied ships after Leyte Gulf, but none of them launched from carriers. The IJN had the ships and planes, but not the carrier-qualified pilots.

Following Leyte Gulf the Japanese Navy could only hide out of range and the U.S. range was creeping north. There was a concerted Allied effort to hunt, locate and destroy Japanese warships. BB *Haruna* limping to safety in French Indo-China, 30 December 1944.

She was being escorted by a leading DD, a DD and two DDE alongside, two tankers travelling in shallower water, and a light cruiser bringing up the rear.

(Inset) Enlargement of *Haruna* on 30 December 1944. Trailing oil, the damaged survivor of Leyte Gulf was photographed off Cap Saint Jacques (Vung Tau, French Indo China) probably on the way to the huge anchorage at Cam Ranh Bay. The taking organization was 444th Bomb Group which flew B-29s out of India.

(Above) Heavy Cruiser *Nachi* being attacked by planes from USS *Essex* on 5 November 1944. She was sunk a few minutes later by *Lexington* aircraft.

USN targets were becoming smaller warships. (Below) A destroyer identified as *Hatsuharu* (actually *Hatsumaru*) sunk off Luzon 13 November 1944. Photo is from a USN ship after Allied reoccupation of the Philippines.

(Above) Another post-war photo shows Light Cruiser *Kiso* (identified by her characteristic "onion" stacks) sunk in shallow water north of Manila in the 13 November 1944 sweep by aircraft from Task Force 58. Her turrets and parts of the superstructure have already been removed, presumably by locals and apparently for salvage.

Still more small vessels and a long string of merchant ships were sunk by the ever expanding and increasingly effective force of USN submarines. Below is a periscope photo of IJN *Patrol Boat #39* (formerly destroyer *Tade*) sinking NE of Formosa on 23 April 1943.

On 1 November 1944 an American aircraft was over Tokyo for the first time since the Doolittle Raid in 1942. It was a lone long-range F-13 (recon B-29) flying from Saipan/Tinian collecting weather Intel, radar and visual imagery. From this day on, no IJN base was out of range. An enlargement of 11 November imagery from a similar recon sortie (below) shows the important IJN Yokosuka Naval Base on southwestern Tokyo Bay. The carrier off shore is probably new 872 foot long "super carrier" *Shinano* (possibly the only U.S. photo of her). There are also three early-1900s battleships in this photo—can you find them?

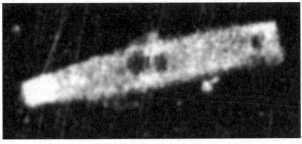

A maximum enlargement of the 11 November imagery shows *Shinano* five weeks after launching and eight days prior to commissioning. She was doing sea trials in Tokyo Bay. Her elevators were down but there were no aircraft in sight.

Allied Intelligence could learn several things about this warship from the photo. Using the camera focal length, aircraft altitude and measurement of the image on the original film, the length and width could be calculated with considerable precision. From that, Naval Analysts could estimate the probable displacement and potential performance.

Shinano was secretly built at Yokosuka Naval Base, in the large empty graving dock seen at lower left in the previous photo, using the third Yamato-class hull. Eighteen days after this photo, on her way to Kure Naval Base in southern Japan, *Shinano* became the largest ship ever sunk by a submarine. Torpedoes from USS *Archerfish* sent her to the bottom in deep water—and she never launched a plane.

(Below) Seven days earlier an F-13 at 33,500 feet over northwest Tokyo (at the location of the large arrow) took this radar scope-photo of Tokyo Bay. Shinano was certainly down there, and large enough to give a return—but without movement between comparative coverage, US analysts probably wouldn't have recognized her as a carrier. The smaller arrow indicates Yokosuka Naval Base.

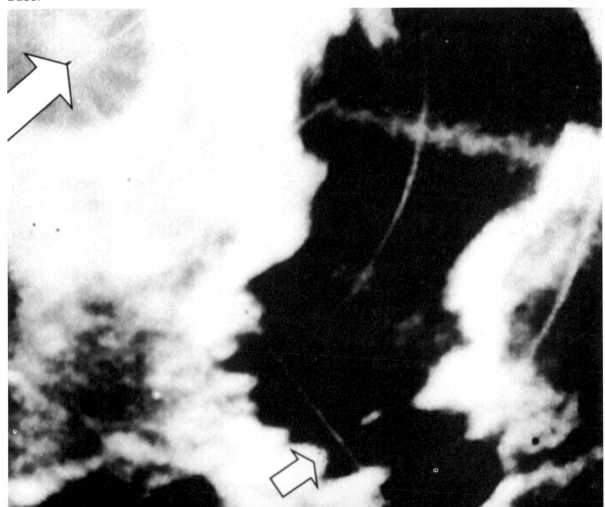

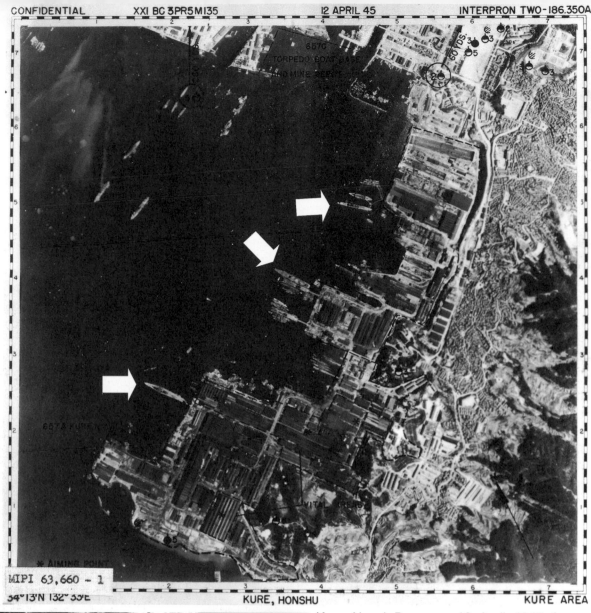

MIPI 63,660 - 1

34°13'N 132°33'E KURE, HONSHU KURE AREA

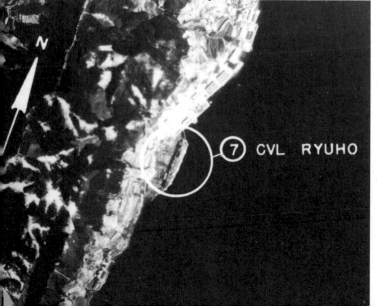

7 CVL RYUHO

Kure Naval Base on 12 April 1945 from a Saipan-based 3rd Photo Squadron F-13. A battleship, carrier, heavy cruiser, and other warships (my arrows), aren't even annotated. Emphasis is on bombing targets in preparation for possible invasion as U.S. B-29s from Tinian, China and planes from Task Force 58 carriers were reaching out to mainland Japan itself.

There was no more "out of range," all the IJN could do was hide—and they were sometimes quite good at that. But U.S. photo interpreters were also good at their craft. The light carrier *Ryuho* was identified near Kure.

(Below Right) Except perhaps to obscure their specific identity it's hard to see what camouflage accomplished for these carriers located near Sasebo in 1945. The PI work for this report wasn't perfect. *Hayataka* didn't exist—it was possibly torpedo-damaged *Junyo*. CV *Kasagi* was incomplete. The ship marked CVL was probably CVE *Ibuki*, also incomplete. The Allies didn't know it yet but IJN carrier-based aviation was finished.

(Below Left) Enlargement of 2 July 45 imagery covering the same location showed carriers covered in netting that reached to the water in some cases. The outline of the CVE was altered, but there is no doubt that all three are aircraft carriers, the natural enemy of a carrier pilot. I don't know why the plane elevators are down on two of the ships, but it made positive ID of a carrier easier.

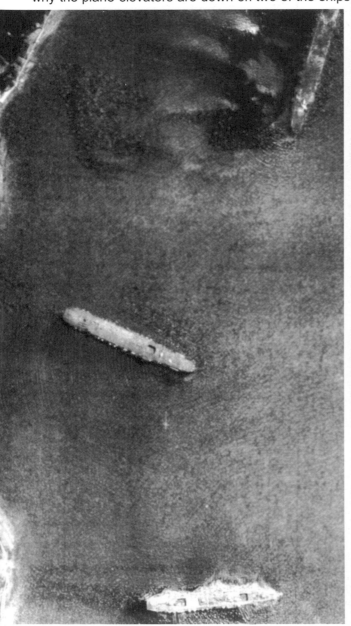

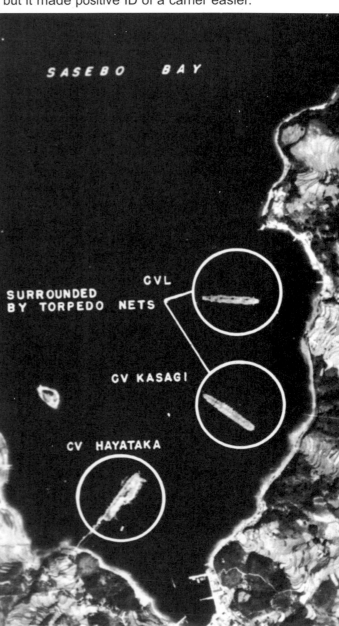

231

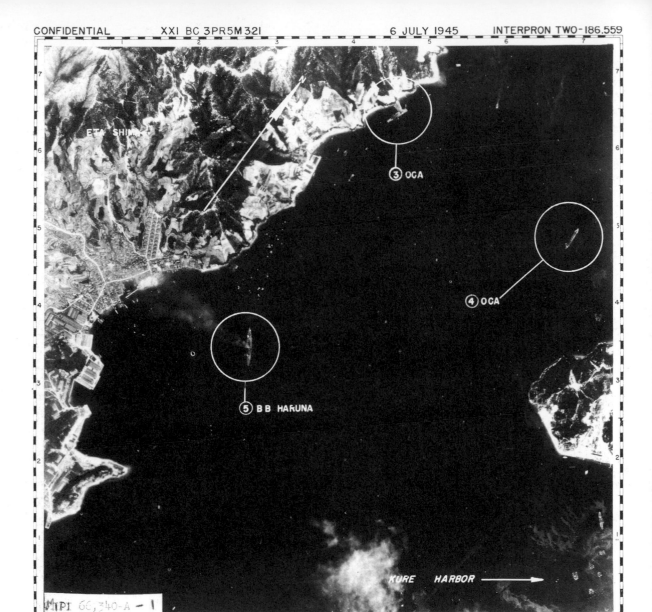

ETA SHIMA

③ OCA

④ OCA

⑤ B B HARUNA

KURE HARBOR →

TPI 66,340-A - 1

34° 15' N. 132° 31' E.   KURE, HONSHU   90.30 - SHIPPING TARGETS

After battle damage during Leyte Gulf, running onto a reef in Malaysia and being attacked by USN subs, Battleship *Haruna*, above, finally made it north to Kure for repairs in early July. I can't identify the two heavily netted "OCA" vessels, but they are both around 400' in length.

Not realizing IJN carrier aviation was exhausted, through war's end even small carriers were sought out by USN aircraft. (Right) Shape and configuration suggest this in *Unyo*, a 591' long CVE sunk by a sub SE of Hong Kong in September 1944.

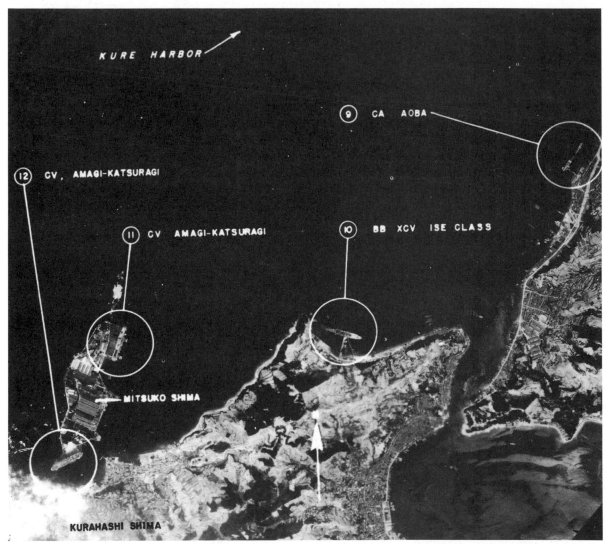

KURE HARBOR

⑨ CA AOBA

⑫ CV, AMAGI-KATSURAGI

⑪ CV AMAGI-KATSURAGI

⑩ BB XCV ISE CLASS

MITSUKO SHIMA

KURAHASHI SHIMA

(Above) Kure Harbor is to the upper right. A small island (Mitsuko Shima) had been extensively camouflaged to change its shape which now also incorporates the hulls of two *Unryu*-class aircraft carriers. The camouflage was good, but not good enough. Following the outlines of the larger island, the ruse would have been easy to detect, and once penetrated the shapes of the carriers were identified. Cruiser *Aoba* wasn't hidden, nor was the old Battleship *Ise*, and that may have served to draw attention to this area. *Ise* shows removal of her after turrets and installation of a short flight deck like her sister ship, *Hyuga* (also at Kure). The so-called hybrid or hermaphrodite carriers were created in 1943/44 to compensate for carrier losses at Midway. I don't believe either ship ever launched a combat sortie from her deck.

(Right) Possibly tanker *Shimane Maru* being converted into a small carrier, 30 July 45 (no location given). Netting is in place to mask work in progress.

233

GÖTTERDÄMMERUNG

Wrong people, wrong navy, wrong side of the world, but a full-blown "Twilight of the Gods" occurred on 6-7 April 1945 south of the island of Kyushu. With no hope of victory, the remains of the IJN (with reduced crews), led by *Yamato*, sortied against U.S. forces engaged in the conquest of Okinawa. That island was considered part of Japan and to not respond to the invasion was unthinkable even though the ten IJN warships were hopelessly outnumbered and without adequate air cover. The best they could foresee was to do as much damage as possible, then beach the huge battleship to act as an "unsinkable gun platform." Japanese warships didn't even have enough fuel to return to home ports. Most of the personnel involved had experienced USN carrier air five months earlier in the Philippines so they knew what to expect. They were facing eleven enemy carriers carrying nearly 400 planes, yet they went.

The suicide sortie was detected by USN subs on the 6 April and scout planes found them the next morning, still well short of Okinawa. Air attacks began shortly after noon.

This photo of *Yamato* in a hard turn to starboard was apparently taken out the back of the turret of a Grumman "Avenger" torpedo-bomber, probably before 1300 hrs local as annotated because the Light Cruiser *Yahagi* (on an opposite course to the battleship) shows no sign of damage. That dot in the clear area above *Yamato* is a Curtis "Helldiver" attacking. Titling on the neg I found was incomplete but I believe it is from *Yorktown* or *Essex* because other photos from those carriers display the same dirt and smears (we used to call it "monkey dung") resulting from hasty processing with improperly cleaned equipment. If from a *Yorktown* aircraft, the time-line of who attacked when needs to be revisited.

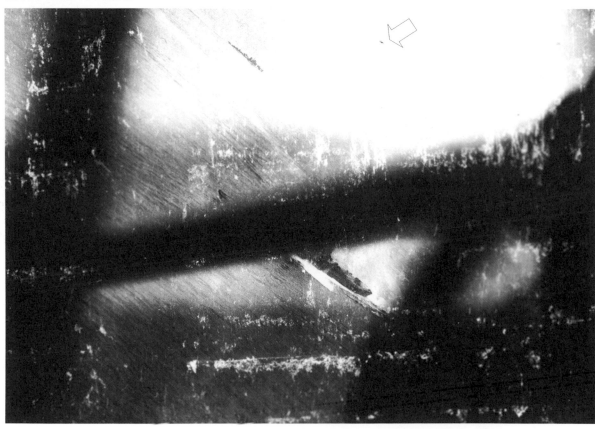

234

Another photo from the same "Avenger" a second later, the attacking aircraft overhead is "boring in" in spite of flak and *Yamato* is still turning. I see no splashes in the water and no apparent damage to the ship, but there is a hint of smoke on the port side between the stack and after main-turret.

The accompanying light cruiser is a faint silhouette (almost behind the ball-turret frame at upper left) and drifting smoke at lower right indicates the position of one of the escorting destroyers (at least two of the eight were sunk by this time). Near the upper right of the photo is a shape that is tantalizingly like an aircraft heading away and banking to the right—it isn't. Extreme enlargement shows it to be a convergence of a flak burst and more "monkey dung."

235

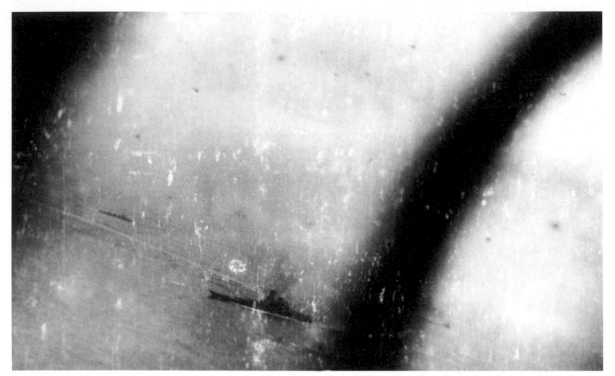

Above, another fast cycle of the film and shutter (which had to be cocked and fired by hand for each exposure) and we see *Yamato* seeming to straighten course with CL *Yahagi* just up and to the left. The cruiser doesn't seem to be leaving as much of a wake as before (compare with the wake of the DD). Is she slowing to turn to a new position beside the battleship to provide better AAA support, or has she been damaged?

Almost behind the BB, on the other side of the aircraft canopy frame, is the closest destroyer. In the air overhead are at least four "Helldivers" that appear to be banking to the right, positioning for dive-bombing runs (or even horizontal bombing attacks).

Then it was CL *Yahagi*'s turn. A *Yorktown* plane photographed her dead in the water (no bow wave or wake) and being bombed. She seems to be on fire amidships.

(Below) A *Yorktown* "Avenger" is circling down for a torpedo run, but *Yahagi* was already done for (smoke and oil slick) and going under. The characteristic pitot-tube at lower left identifies the "taking" aircraft for this and the photo above as another "Avenger."

As the attack continued everything was concentrated on *Yamato*. The photo below shows the BB (center right) low at the stern and smoking. That ship engulfed in black smoke at left center may be DD *Suzutsuki*. The tall column of white smoke just behind the DD may be what's left of the light cruiser. They both sank just after 1400 hrs. An unscathed destroyer is ahead of the stricken BB and on the same course (heading to the left).

(Below) Two hours of pounding and *Yamato* was dead in the water from twelve torpedo and seven 1000 lb. bomb hits (some sources say 12 bombs and seven torpedoes). There is an extensive oil slick ahead and behind the battleship and no apparent wake. On fire and lower at the stern, *Yamato* was starting to capsize when she experienced the first of several internal explosions—this one caught by a *Yorktown* aircraft.

(Above) An *Essex* "Helldiver" photographed what may be *Yamato's* last moments. Some of her superstructure appears still above water. A surviving DD shows just to the left of the smoke column and another is below the propeller of the "Helldiver."

A second later *Yamato* was rolling and going under as the *Essex* "Helldiver" pulls even with his Squadron-mate. For years I have looked at this photo under the highest magnification I could achieve (and the film would take) and I'm convinced that pilot is looking at the camera, not the sinking ship—and he's grinning.

238

(Below) A *Yorktown* "Avenger" photographed what may be the final explosion (which occurred underwater) though under high magnification some of the hull aft of the stack seems above water. Perhaps I should have put this photo earlier in the sequence?

A lone DD is heeling in a hard turn and there are no aircraft in the sky nearby. Apparently everyone knew the day was over. There is nothing like the threat of a large explosion to clear the air-space.

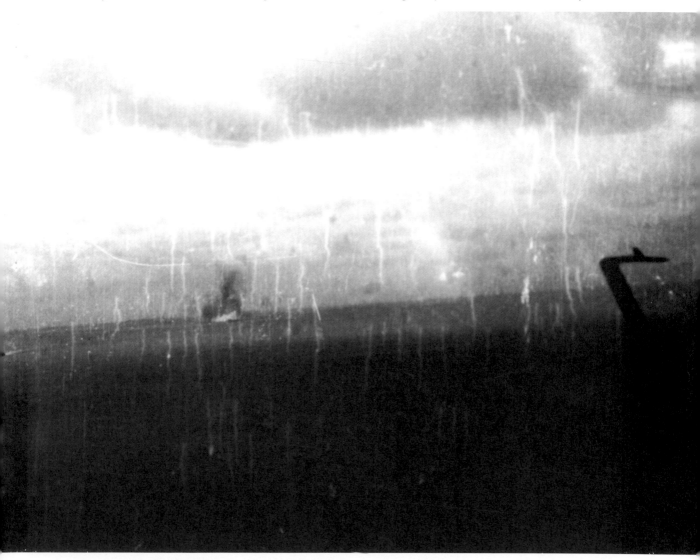

The great ship went down with only 280 crewmen to be rescued by the two surviving DDs. Imperial Japanese Navy honor had been served.

The largest, most heavily armed and armored battleship ever built was gone and the age of big-gun ship-to-ship naval warfare begun 500 years earlier was clearly over. The end was begun by Brig. Gen. Billy Mitchell in the 1920s, confirmed by *Bismarck*, at Taranto and Pearl Harbor, underlined by Leyte Gulf and here north of Okinawa. Battleships provided more useful service as floating gun platforms but carrier aviation now ruled over the gun-ship in sea warfare.

239

THE REST OF THE WAR—AND AFTER

After Leyte Gulf the IJN had it worse than the USN had suffered in early 1942. There were no more victories, and any ship venturing forth had a high probability of being sunk. In addition to naval air, USN submarines had increased in numbers, honed their skills, and forged a tightening ring around Japan and her remaining bases. In addition to sinking Japanese ships, they reported locations for others to attack. By 1945 no place was out of range and there was no place to shelter or hide.

On 24 July 45, USN Task Force 58 planes swept into the huge harbor at Kure, going after the core of what was left of the IJN. This is hybrid BB *Hyuga*.

Hyuga leaking oil and on the bottom just off shore sometime after the attack. The midships twin turrets of her WW I heritage are almost under water and her make-shift flight deck is a shambles showing hits by at least two large bombs.

(Above) Sister hybrid Battleship *Ise* seen from the back seat of a *Lexington* "Helldiver" during the same 24 July attack. The oval disruption of water is typical of a torpedo hit. She looks low in the bow already so this was probably not the first wave of attackers.

Ise survived the Kure attack and tried to run but was caught by USN carrier planes and sunk four days later about five miles NW of Kure.

The next two photos show a much damaged Battleship *Nagato* at Kure. Faint hand-titling (below) indicates a date sometime in August 1945. Sailors can be seen on deck and she's riding high in the water but the foremast and midships are a wreck. The aft-mast is missing as is the top of the funnel and the hull looks like she's seen some hard days. Characteristic dive-brakes show the taking aircraft was a Curtis SB2C "Helldiver" and titling says it flew off USS *Essex*.

(Above) Yokosuka Naval Base, 31 May 45. Three cruisers and several DD are moored here along with a very well camouflaged BB *Nagato* (arrow). The large empty graving-dock up and to the right of the BB is where the giant CV *Shinano* was built in secret.

243

Still at Yokosuka on 31 May 1945—there are three old battleships/armored cruisers in this photo. At upper right may be *Azuma* (1900), Center left is *Kasuga* (1904). Bottom left, the ship on land is *Mikasa* (1902), Admiral Togo's flagship during the great 1905 sea battle in Tsushima Straits that defeated the Czarist fleet during the Russo-Japanese War. *Mikasa* was moved on shore and set in concrete as a memorial in 1926 and to avoid the BB being counted in Washington Naval Treaty quotas. After WW II the Soviets wanted *Mikasa* destroyed but cooler heads prevailed and the historic old warship was saved.

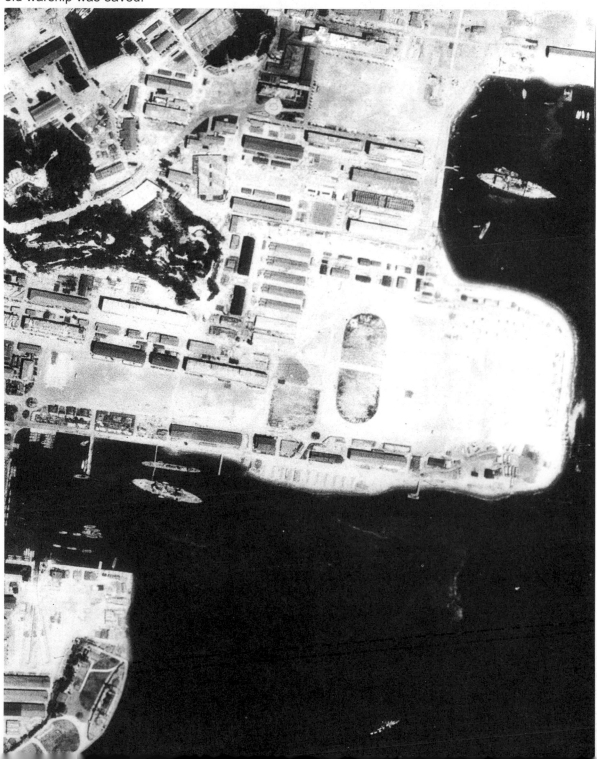

(Above) The same area after the war with the two relatively harmless old warships sunk by USN carrier aircraft on 18 July 1945. The historic *Mikasa* is untouched in the foreground. (while stationed in Japan, I first toured her there in 1960)

(Left) It seems an American service man salvaged/ appropriated an IJN suicide boat (possibly a *Shinyo* Type 2) for recreation.

245

(Above) Yokosuka Naval Base on 20 May 1947 with surrendered destroyers, mine-layers and patrol boats lined up for disposition.

(Below) Kure Naval Base after the war with surrendered ships anchored but still manned—note canvas awnings rigged on decks for crewmen. There are small and large destroyers, at least one light cruiser, an old armored cruiser, numerous patrol craft and mine-layers, and a good selection of submarines (nearest the camera), including some really big ones—one at left center has deck containers that may have been to carry float-planes.

Sasebo Bay was a jackpot of large ships on 26 September 1945. The carrier at right is probably incomplete *Ibuki*. The other carrier is incomplete *Kasagi*.

(Below) Another look at *Kasagi*. This was the perfect metaphor for the Imperial Japanese Navy in mid-1945—anchored in port, incomplete and impossible to equip and man operationally. The sub on the left is probably *Ha.201* and on the right may be *I.58*.

FOOTNOTES

[1]Soviet agent Richard Sorge was picking up a lot on Japanese "intentions" while posing as a Nazi, but the Soviets weren't sharing the intelligence with the West.

[2]The first surface-to-surface engagement occurred in the Solomon's in November 1942. I discount the February-March loss of CAs USS *Houston* and HMS *Exeter* (veteran of *Graf Spee* sinking); CLs HMAS *Perth*, HM *de Ruyter*, and *Java*; and most of their escorting destroyers off the Netherlands East Indies because the survivors were captured and no Allied analysis of the engagement could be made until their recovery late in the war.

[3]All but two of the Pearl Harbor casualties were eventually returned to service but for well over a year the IJN had a significant numerical superiority in Battleships.

[4]Discounting AV-3, *Langley* (ex-CV-1). Four more USN CV were in the Atlantic.

[5]Japanese fighters and bombers at Rabaul had longer range than the planes initially based on Guadalcanal but B-17s could "stage" through from Australia.

[6]Perhaps it was the Samurai tradition (I lived in Japan for eight years and know a little about that), but Japan had tried mult-prong offensive operations like this in China since 1937. Wake Island, various actions in the Solomon's and New Guinea are other examples, but they never seemed to learn—it only worked when they had surprise or overwhelming superiority to cover up poor timing, as early in the war.

[7]*Jane's* for 1943-44 didn't know about them but anticipated construction of several 16" gun battleships.

[8]*Iowa*-class BBs were 20 K tons lighter, at least five knots faster, slightly longer, slightly less beam (because of Panama Canal lock restrictions) and armed with nine 16" guns in three turrets that ranged with the Japanese guns albeit without the projectile volley weight. I don't believe *Musashi* ever fired her main batteries at an enemy target and *Yamato* only did once.

[9]There may have been many other negatives from this battle in boxes I didn't screen during my three years of randomly searching through retired DoD Intel photo files.

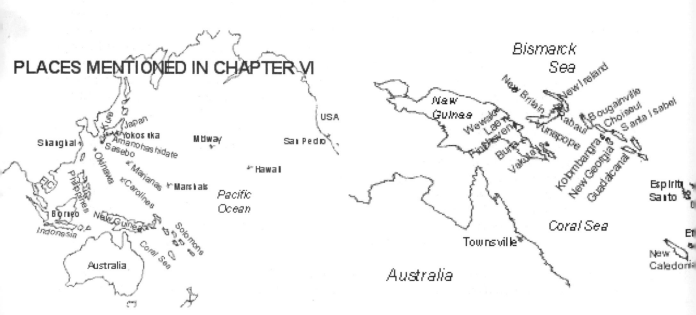

PLACES MENTIONED IN CHAPTER VI

248

CHAPTER VII
FINAL OBSERVATIONS

Once again I remind the reader that this is a collection of photographs that caught my eye while screening retired Intelligence files, my photo interpretation and my opinions. The text isn't intended to be a complete or comprehensive history of the war, a fleet, a navy, or individual ships. It is my relating what I see in the photographs (with a little help from my library of WW II books and the internet). Drawing upon experience as a PI and Intel Analyist, I want to end this work with some general conclusions/opinions that evolved over the several decades of looking at these photos and the several years of putting the book together.

Both the Allies and France were fortunate that French warships remained largely out of Axis control. They would certainly have tilted the balance in the Mediterranean, likely forcing more Royal Navy assets shifted from critical duty in the Atlantic. Given the circumstances of 1940, Mers el Kebir was unfortunate but necessary. Scuttling at Toulon in the face of German occupation was a bold and courageous act, and the right thing to do for France.

Mussolini's fleet was designed for swift aggressive offensive action but they ran head-on into a Navy that was more aggressive, more determined and better led. Smacked hard at Taranto and Matapan, they were forced onto the defensive, such as convoy escort, early in the war. Unable to perform as intended (in part because of poor leadership, poor reconnaissance, and poor air-sea coordination), major units of the Italian Navy wound up in port, still a threat but essentially dormant.

The German Navy was a classic example of a military force crippled by an absolute dictator making the wrong decisions again and again, in part because he never really understood naval warfare. The few large new surface warships were magnificent machines but cool heads must have known (particularly after the loss of *Bismarck*) that there was no way to successfully employ them (i.e., expose them to direct enemy action) for any length of time. Oh, they caused a lot of anguish in Allied Naval HQ and did considerable damage to Allied shipping, but it was as an ambusher, darting out to strike then hurrying back to the relative safety of distance and an air umbrella. The heavy, counterpart Allied ships they tied up were mainly warships that weren't involved in anti-submarine warfare—and *U*-boats were the most pressing danger. The men and materials committed to ships such as *Tirpitz* could have built and crewed dozens of *U*-Boats which would have had a better chance of being decisive. Submarines were relatively cheap and could be built rapidly in small shipyards, dispersing construction, making it almost impossible for the RAF (and later USAAF) to interdict. I remember as a boy seeing little boat yards all along Lake Michigan quickly shifted from building pleasure and fishing boats before the war to making small wood-hull Subchasers and Mine Sweepers. Much the same thing could have been done for *U*-boats using small boat yards all along the Baltic coast such as done at Stettin. I believe I know what would have happened if in 1936 Hitler had elected to concentrate his naval construction on U-Boats.

The Imperial Japanese Navy learned the tactical lesson of Taranto and executed it well at Pearl Harbor, but apparently didn't grasp that the strategic situation was very different so they concentrated on the wrong targets. Despite the limited capability for retaliation by U.S. Forces still operational on Oahu after 7 December, the IJN didn't follow-up with a second air attack to destroy the right objectives.

Desperate for a respite, the Royal Navy bought time at Taranto when twenty-two carrier-based bi-planes sank Italian warships in shallow water—but didn't destroy them. The IJN should have understood that lesson. Seven of the eight Pearl Harbor casualties took part in combat later in the war. After the initial attack virtually eliminated the possibility of U.S. fighter or bomber opposition, the overwhelming strength of Japanese battleships and carriers could have advanced within gun range of Pearl Harbor and picked off surviving USN warships as they exited the channel for open sea. At the very least they should have launched air attacks until Pearl Harbor was eliminated as a base. Admittedly the IJN commanders were concerned because they didn't know the location of the two missing USN carriers, but they had six CV and 420 planes, and a demonstrably superior fighter and aerial torpedo capability. The first carrier vs. carrier battle was still six months away so no one knew what might happen, but those odds seem like a comfortable advantage.

Another reason fixating on USN Battleships was a tactical error, had not a single BB been sunk in their berths but oil storage and ship repair facilities and supplies destroyed, the U.S. Pacific Fleet would have been forced back to the West Coast. Resulting long sorties into the Central or Western Pacific, far beyond air cover, would have been vulnerable to IJN submarines. Rebuilding and refilling the fuel tanks would have taken months and made USN tankers vulnerable to IJN submarines (and the *I-boats* were excellent long distance subs).

West Coast basing would have meant USN subs and carriers had less operational time on the far side of the Pacific. Surface engagements would have been more hazardous for the USN (even the rebuilt IJN battleships were as well-gunned and up to five to ten knots faster than USN counterparts until the *Iowa*-class). As proven with HMS *Prince of Wales* and *Repulse*, deep water sinkings were final.

Drawing the American Navy west to rescue the Philippines (which was actually one of the pre-war U.S. War Plans) would have put those ships under substantial land based air attack with no air support of their own except from carriers. Tying carriers to the battleship defense would have sacrificed much of their speed, mobility and flexibility (much like misuse of Luftwaffe fighters as bomber escorts in the fall of 1940), diminishing their effectiveness.[1] As events played out, many U.S. Admirals may not have liked it but Pearl Harbor losses forced them into an air-centric land and sea war style at which the USN quickly excelled. The IJN was on the defensive from mid-1942 on, unable to effectively replace ship and pilot losses[2]—rendering them unable to counter erosion of far-flung land forces.

Japanese submarines accomplished nothing like they might have with a more vigorous building program.[3] IJN had several classes of subs over 300' long and with over 20 knot speed on the surface. They had undersea boats that carried aircraft, suicide manned torpedoes and heavy equipment as deck-loads. Japanese subs also had the best torpedo in the war. Many were long-ranged, fast under water, and some were highly innovative in design (such as *I-201*), but the best ones were too few and came too late in the war to change things. Meanwhile, they had to contend with USN subs and anti-submarine hunter forces, armed with the latest sub-killer weapons, guided by SONAR and radar systems that were getting better and better. By 1944 Allied warships and planes were quite good at sinking enemy submarines. Meanwhile, the sheer number of defenders and hunters around the most lucrative Allied surface targets kept IJN subs from racking up the successes USN submarines in "wolf-packs" were having against lone targets and small convoys.

Dear Reader: I hope you enjoy these photos as much as I enjoyed putting the book together.

FOOTNOTES

[1]The USN carriers in the Pacific on 7 December 1941 were capable of speeds ten knots faster than the WWI vintage BB stationed at Pearl Harbor.

[2]The IJN only introduced one new BB during the war and two CV, six CVL and two CVE (none of the carriers took part in a battle).

[3]IJN SS only managed to sink USN CVs *Wasp* and *Yorktown* (already crippled by air attack), one CVE and two CA.

BIBLIOGRAPHY

Babington-Smith, Flight Officer Constance, WAAF. Air Spy. New York, N.Y.: Ballantine Books, 1957. Paperback ed.

Brookes, Andrew J. Photo Reconnaissance. London, England: Ian Allan Ltd., 1975.

Carter, Kit C. and Mueller, Robert, compilers. Army Air Forces in World War II: Combat Chronology 1941-1945. Washington, DC: Office of Air Force History, 1973.

Craven, Wesley F. and Cate, James L. The Army Air Forces in World War II, vol. 3. Washington, D.C.: Office of Air Force History, 1983.

Der Zweite Weltkrieg Im Bild, Band II. Baden-Baden, GR: Eilebrect (compilation of photos included as sales inducements in cigarette packages), circa late 1940s.

"Evidence In Camera," ACIU magazine, March 1945 special edition reprinted by Medmenham Club.

Falk, Stanley L. Decision At Leyte. New York, N.Y.: Berkley Publishing Corp., 1966.

Forester, C. S. Sink the Bismarck! New York, N.Y.: Bantam Books, 1959.

Hastings, Max. Bomber Command. New York, N.Y.: The Dial Press, 1979.

Hinsley, F. H. British Intelligence in the Second World War, vol.1, 2 & 3. New York, N.Y.: Cambridge University Press, 1979, 1981 & 1984.

Jane's Fighting Ships 1943-4. New York, N.Y.: Mcmillian Co., 1945.

Jentschura, Hansgerog, Jung, Dieter and Mickel, Peter. Warships of the Imperial Japanese Novy, 1869-1945. London, England: Arms and Armour Press, 1977. This book is a MUST for anyone doing research on the IJN.

Keegan, John. Intelligence in War. New York, N.Y.: Vintage Books, 2004.

Kreis, John F. (Gen Ed.). Piercing the Fog. Washington, D.C., Air Force and Museums Program, 1996.

Lewin, Ronald. Ultra Goes to War. New York, N.Y.: Pocket Books, 1978.

Morrison, Adm. Samuel Eliot. The Two Ocean War. Boston, Mass.: Little, Brown and Company, 1963.

Nesbit, Roy Conyers. Eyes of the RAF. Phoenix Mill, Gloucestershire, England: Alan Sutton Publishing Limited, 1996.

Powell, Michael. Death in the South Atlantic. New York, N.Y.: Ace Books, Inc., 1957

Powys-Lybbe, Flight Officer Ursula, WAAF. The Eye of Intelligence. London, England: William Kimber & Co. Limited, 1983.

Price, Dr. Alfred. Targeting the Reich. London, England: Greenhill Books, 2003.

Robertson, Terence. Channel Dash. New York, N.Y.: Berkley Books, 1958.

Staesck, Chris, ed. Allied Photo Reconnaissance of World War Two. San Diego, CA: Thunder Bay Press, 1998.

251

Stanley, Col. Roy M. II, USAF (ret.) To Fool A Glass Eye. Shrewsbury, UK: Airlife Publishing Ltd., 1998.

———- World War II Photo Intelligence. New York, N.Y.: Charles Scribner's Sons, 1981.

Webster, Sir Charles and Frankland, Noble. The Strategic Air Offensive Against Germany 1939-1945 (four volumes). London, England: Her Majesty's Stationary Office, 1961.

Welchman, Gordon. The Hut Six Story. New York, N.Y.: McGraw-Hill Book Company, 1982.

Woodward, C. Vann. The Battle For Leyte Gulf. New York, N.Y.: The Macmillan Company, 1947.

World Naval Ship Forum internet site

INDEX

254